5/05

Jeremy Horner

# ISLAND DREAMS
# MEDITERRANEAN

with 246 color illustrations

Thames & Hudson

**In memory of Maria Grazia Cutuli,
a Sicilian treasure**

*Half-title* Fishermen on the north-west coast
of Djerba, Tunisia.

*Frontispiece* Quintessential Mediterranean:
the streets of Mykonos, Greece.

First published in 2004 in hardcover in the United States of
America by Thames & Hudson Inc., 500 Fifth Avenue,
New York, New York 10110

thamesandhudsonusa.com

Library of Congress Catalog Card Number 2004100252
ISBN 0-500-51176-4

Printed and bound in China by Toppan.

# CONTENTS

porquerolles
france p32
mallorca
ibiza
spanish islands p12
tunisia p176

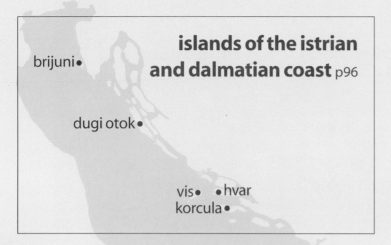

**islands of the istrian
and dalmatian coast** p96

brijuni•

dugi otok•

vis• •hvar
korcula•

**bay of naples
& pontine islands** p42

ischia• •procida
capri•

**lian islands** p70

lipari•
•vulcano

•mo
gnana•

gozo•

**malta** p188

**greek islands** p128

corfu•

zakynthos•

•mykonos

symi•

santorini•

•rhodes

Rural life still flourishes in Mallorca, in spite of the tourist influx.

Day-trippers gather in the Piazza Umberto I in the old town of Capri.

Habitats of the gods and heroes of the ancient world, quiet hideaways from the pressures of urban mainland living, or settings for the unbridled pursuit of pleasure, the islands of the Mediterranean enjoy a richness beyond compare in their history, their scenery, and in their villages and towns. Small wonder, then, that for centuries many were regarded as among the most important centres of the civilized world and exercised an irresistible attraction for the inhabitants of lands less fortunately endowed. That attraction is still as intense today as it ever was, making the selection of twenty or so islands to express the spirit of 'the Mediterranean island' a particularly daunting task, but also an enthralling one.

One major consideration was that all the places included should express 'islandness' – that is, that however well-known they may be, they should still evoke the image of faraway destinations, romance and adventure always suggested by the word 'islands'. Hence, it was decided not to include any of the larger islands; Corsica, Sardinia, Crete, Sicily and Cyprus, for instance, are substantial entities in their own right, without

the sense of individuality immediately felt on smaller islands, like the Egadi, Aeolian or Cyclades.

Along with individuality, a surviving identity expressed in the indelible imprint of history characterizes the final choice; these are islands with a kind of indigenous strength and spirit which have survived beneath the overlays of mass-tourism and residential developments, where local communities are still living and vibrant. Some have been known as holiday destinations for decades, such as Capri and a number of the Greek islands, while others are just emerging as possibilities – at least for travellers from northern Europe and America.

All the main island groups of the Mediterranean are represented, moving roughly in an eastward direction, plus a number of 'could-not-be-excluded' individual cases: Porquerolles, distinctive for having resisted the over-development which has engulfed the rest of the Riviera; Djerba, off the coast of Tunisia, which still retains vigorous traditional elements in its various communities, in spite of having given up one entire coastline to the needs of holidaymakers; peaceful Gozo, where

Ponza, in the Pontine Islands, attracts a discerning class of summer visitors and residents.

Vis is the furthest-flung of the Croatian islands.

the visitor may feel free from any pressure to conduct matters at more than a strolling pace; Ibiza, where a tranquil interior offers respite from the animated tourist traps; and Mallorca, where a rural idyll is only a few kilometres from sophisticated city life.

Apart from these cases, the islands included here fall into three distinct groups: the Italian, including the Aeolian, the Egadi, the Pontine and those of the Bay of Naples; the islands of the Istrian and Dalmatian coasts, whose beauty and variety are at last becoming widely known; and the Greek islands, both familiar and less familiar. But whether falling within one of these groups, with related networks of ferry and hydrofoil services, or individual and more isolated, all the islands here offer richness and variety – scenic, cultural and sporting. And they are all, in their own ways, extremely beautiful.

Within the major groups, of course, the process of selection was almost as arduous as that for the Mediterranean as a whole. Leaving aside the Greek islands, long known to generations of visitors from overseas, the main problems of choice were presented by the Italian islands which – apart from those in the Bay of Naples – have never figured too prominently on the major tourist routes, and those off the Istrian and Dalmatian coasts of the former Yugoslavia. Again, among well-defined groupings like the archipelagoes in the seas west of the Italian mainland and Sicily, picking out individual islands always meant that another with a pressing case for inclusion had to be omitted. So many of the Pontine, Aeolian and Egadi groups have distinct and unique natural attractions, both of coastline and interior, coupled with local life of colour and energy centred almost without exception on a working harbour and its related town or village. How powerful is that vision of a row of weathered façades in faded white, yellow and pink grouped around a quayside, or of small-town piazzas, surrounded by shops, cafés and restaurants!

Of all the Italian islands, it was probably Ponza which corresponded most closely to the classic vision evoked by the phrase 'Mediterranean island'; if there had been any doubts about its inclusion, these were rapidly seen off by the fact that it is also blessed with one of the finest beaches of the whole

Graceful neoclassical architecture characterizes many of the streets of the old town of Corfu.

Local residents relax in the early morning shade on Mykonos.

Mediterranean, the Chiaia di Luna. The main islands off Naples, Capri and Ischia, could hardly be left out; they are both of great beauty in their very different ways and, although on every well-beaten tourist route, offer satisfactions for every taste from the gregarious to the reclusive. Any book on Mediterranean islands would have seemed perversely toothless without them. The third island of that hallowed bay, Procida, is less visited by tourist crowds, leaving its population of fisherfolk to go about its business from the picturesque little harbour of Corricella, lined by the slightly dilapidated balconied houses which provided such an engaging background to many of the unbearably touching scenes in the film classic, *Il Postino*.

West of Sicily lies the mini-archipelago of the Egadi Islands, whose inhabitants enjoy a rich heritage from both Italian and Arab cultures. Favignana and tiny Marettimo support active fishing fleets and thrive on a sense of the continuity of Mediterranean life. There is an abiding sense here of the rhythms and rituals of seasonal activities in fishing and in cultivation. The event of the year on Favignana is La Mattanza, the massive cull of tuna fish

as they return to their breeding grounds in late spring – a particularly bloody spectacle, carried out in age-old fashion to the accompaniment of traditional chants.

Home to the classical god of the winds, the Aeolian Islands are essentially volcanoes in the sea; in fact, one of them, Stromboli, is Europe's most continuously active volcano. Because its attractions depend so much on the pyrotechnics associated with its enormous crater, it was decided to opt here for the more developed pleasures of Lipari and Vulcano, although the latter is possessed of an impressive crater and enough thermal springs and mud baths to satisfy the most ardent searcher after extreme natural phenomena. And the main town of Lipari is one of the most perfect island communities of the whole Mediterranean.

The islands of the Croatian coastline have a unique fascination in that for many years they were difficult of access. Those of Brijuni, off the Istrian coast, were the private fiefdom of President Tito; others were militarized zones. But perhaps their relative inaccessibility has contributed to their attractions, particularly that of finding towns of unspoiled splendour: honey-stoned

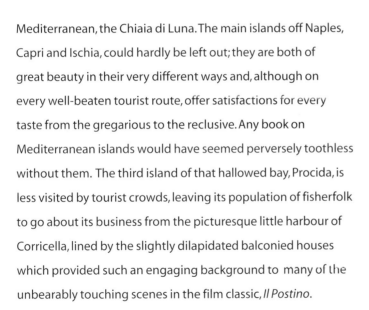

introduction

Elegant Italianate mansions climb the hill behind the harbour of Symi.

The old town of Rhodes is full of fascinating alleys and lanes.

Komiza on the island of Vis; the old walled town of Korcula, with its Venetian palaces; and Hvar, the most elegant island capital in the whole of the Adriatic, again Venetian in appearance, and also possessed of a vibrant social life.

Choosing the Greek islands for inclusion was pretty well the classic impossible task; so many were possible candidates. Keeping in mind, though, the principles of 'most beautiful' and 'most interesting', it seemed appropriate that Corfu and Rhodes should be included, even though some of their more subtle pleasures have been eroded by the tourist invasions. They are both extraordinarily beautiful and possess island capitals of great interest and animation. Zakynthos, in the Ionian Islands, and Santorini, in the Cyclades, are here because of the sheer drama and spectacular character of their topography, and for the sense of 'islandness' they air with peculiar intensity. Mykonos, now much frequented but still of intense charm,

and Symi, with its graceful pastel-coloured houses, complete the group as representatives of contrasting forms of island tourism.

Clearly, this book is not a formal guide, but rather an evocation and celebration of what we understand to be the 'Mediterranean island'. It is with these islands that we associate the most intense images of that sea and its historically charged communities. The Mediterrranean is omnipresent in the dreams of travellers from less favoured climates: sapphire-blue waters, sunshine fading magically into evening balm, olive groves, cypress trees, honey-coloured stone buildings, and vibrant quayside cafés and bars. Add to this vision sandy beaches, rocky coves, picturesque harbours complete with fishing vessels: the result can be observed in many of the images included in the following chapters. No-one would deny that many of the islands have been affected by the demands of mass-tourism, yet in all of those included here indigenous strengths and individualities still proclaim themselves unabashed.

# spanish islands

## ibiza

## mallorca

Mallorca's northern coast is dotted with picturesque villages and small towns, like Llucalcari, a clifftop delight of terracotta roofed houses and a tiny church.

# ibiza

After a period as a fashionable though out-of-the-way destination in the nineteen-sixties and seventies, Ibiza has now become synonymous with youthful hedonism during the summer months. Today, it is home to several of the top club venues in Europe, which attract large numbers of young visitors from all parts of the continent between June and September. Outside this period, however, the island takes on an entirely different mantle, when many hotels and businesses close down for more than half the year. If dancing to the Balearic beat is not your first priority, then this is the time to come to the island to discover the many secret delights of the gently undulating interior and the coves and beaches of the rugged coastline.

The island was an important staging post on the ancient trade routes of the Mediterranean, and under the Romans it enjoyed the special status of 'confederated city'. It came to real prominence under the Moors, who left it with its present name, derived from the Arabic 'Yebisah', and with the distinctive appearance of the old walled town. Inland, the landscape of the island is remarkably endowed with extensive plantations of pine and a wealth of fruit, nut and berry trees, which flourish in the rich brown earth.

Meticulously attended fields of lavender, tomatoes and a smattering of modest vineyards provide yet more variety and colour to a countryside in which farmers can be seen patiently coaxing their strapping ponies into ploughing the fields in scenes seemingly from bygone centuries. And everywhere there is the aroma from the pine forests which, combined with the benevolent climate, makes for a wonderfully soothing environment at the island's heart. Here, too, are scattered a number of picturesque hilltop villages named after saints, each boasting an architecturally unique whitewashed church at its highest point.

The coastline is punctuated by a large number of almost inaccessible coves (*calas*), constantly flushed out by strong currents to create some of the clearest waters of the Mediterranean. Many of the soft golden sandy beaches lapped by those waters are constant recipients of the coveted European Union Blue Flags for excellence. Forty-eight islets add to the coastal spectacle, making these waters a favourite venue for yachtsmen. But whatever activity you choose – or, indeed, if you prefer the option of not doing very much – remember always that Ibiza is for relaxation.

Away from the tourist centres, there is still a traditional rural Ibiza of whitewashed cuboid houses and ancient churches (*opposite* and *above*). A typical house is, literally, a series of cubes, each one of which represents a single room giving on to a central common space.

The old town of Eivissa (*opposite*) still retains much of its medieval character within sixteenth-century walls, originally built on the orders of Charles V. The streets of Ibizan villages are often characterized by fine, handsome houses, fronted by large porches for additional shade, like this example in San Miguel de Balansart (*right* and *below*), in the north of the island.

Although the coast around the bay of Sant Antoni on Ibiza's west coast has been extensively developed to cater for tourists, pockets of a more traditional lifestyle can still be found along its creeks and coves (*opposite*). South of here lie the cliffs of Cala Vedella (*below*), where every sunset appears no less than magnificent.

The pace of life in rural Ibiza is pretty well much as it has been for centuries and a far cry from the throbbing scene of the coastal resorts. Crops include lavender, tomatoes and some vines for wine production. These scenes (*opposite*) show the pleasant landscape around Sant Mateu di Albaca and Santa Agnes de Corona in the island's interior.

Churches on Ibiza reflect the styles of domestic architecture – an interplay of gleaming white exteriors and dark interiors. The basic forms are cuboid, with squarish façades topped by small bell gables. This hill-top church at Santa Eulària des Riu (*right*), said to be the oldest on the island, has all the characteristics of the fort-like construction which often had to serve as the last refuge for a population under constant threat of attack by pirates.

# mallorca

There is a long-standing joke in Spain about the existence of a fifth Balearic island known as 'Majorca' (English spelling) which has a population of eight million tourists! Indeed, Mallorca has seemingly been colonized since the nineteen-sixties by the British, Germans and other northern Europeans. Yet the sheer diversity of this island of beguiling beauty seems somehow to absorb the impact of the tourist visitors to retain its own distinct flavour and personality. Even within an hour of landing at Palma's spacious international airport, you can find yourself faced with a choice of environments as diverse as the city's historical centre, a mountain wilderness, or a secluded fishing cove.

In the fifteenth century Palma was the pre-eminent port for trade between Europe and Africa; the prosperity this status brought to the place is fully reflected in its architecture. Renaissance mansions give the winding streets of the old town a kind of regal charm. The cathedral of La Seu, encased in its gigantic buttresses, rises up magnificently. Deco cafés and fashionable shops line the smarter streets, below the wrought-iron balconies of the apartment blocks above, creating an effect reminiscent of Barcelona or Paris. And today Palma has become once again a thriving city, since gaining a substantial amount of local autonomy in 1983.

Yet, at no great distance northwards from the bustling streets of Palma, it is possible to find oneself enveloped in the serenity of a wooded valley of terraced fields, such as those which surround the country town of Valldemossa. The pure mountain air of the place, the light mist which often lies on the town at dawn and dusk, all combine to produce a sublime sense of tranquillity and stillness. Once visited by Chopin and George Sand (in 1838–39), the Carthusian monastery in the centre of the little town is now Mallorca's most visited building after Palma's cathedral. Other associations have attracted visitors to this part of the north coast. Film actor Michael Douglas has opened a popular nightclub-restaurant in Valldemossa, but the main credit for placing the area indelibly on the visitor's map must surely go to the English writer and poet Robert Graves, who made his home in the exquisite small town of Deià.

Behind the northern shoreline rise the rugged peaks of the Tramuntana, which reaches its highest point at Puig Major

In strict contrast to the vibrant bustle of Palma, Mallorca's capital, are such places as Santanyí, in the south-east corner of the island. Quiet courtyards and a Sunday-morning chat reveal a way of life still robust after years of playing host to tourists from northern Europe (*opposite* and *above*).

(1,436 m/4,771 ft); there are few sights more dramatic than the reddening of the mountain in the late afternoon sun just before it slips below the horizon. The upper slopes of the range are furrowed by valleys of pine, while olive and citrus groves are gathered around the lower flanks, which descend to the turquoise-watered coves, hidden between rocky spurs. This is marvellous walking country, as Archduke Ludwig Salvator (1847–1915) must have discovered, as he explored the island from his home in the valley of Sóller in preparation of his massive compilation of observations on the whole Balearic archipelago.

Mallorca's northern coast reaches its climax at the Cabo de Formentor to form one of the most awesome landscapes in Europe. Here, the mountains plunge down to the sea in a majestic sequence of cliffs, both on the actual coastline and inland. To the south, along the east coast, the island presents yet another of its many fascinating faces: a sequence of cliffs, pitted with coves and caves, seen at their most spectacular in the Coves d'Artà and the Coves del Drach. The many inlets, often lined with luxuriant vegetation, provide perfect shelter for some of the island's smaller fishing communities. Traditional white, single-masted boats dot the blue waters, symbols of the continuing vitality of the island and its indigenous inhabitants, who have never yielded up their regard for the place, in spite of the tourist invasion.

The rocky north-west coast, just a short drive from Palma, is a place of exquisite rural and coastal retreats. Among them is Deià (*opposite*), famous as the long-time home of the English poet Robert Graves and generally favoured by writers and painters. Its terracotta dwellings tumble down its hill in confusion amid olive and almond trees. Just to the south of Deià lies the serene country town of Valldemossa among olive groves and orchards. Its shady main square (*above*) leads to the Carthusian monastery at the heart of the town, which gained some notoriety in 1838–39, when it was visited by Chopin and George Sand.

Mallorca is an island of infinite variety – enough to satisfy the varied tastes of its visitors. Within easy distance of sophisticated and vibrant Palma lie the terracotta roofs of the rural idyll which is Valldemossa.

The narrow streets of Valldemossa may suddenly reveal views of the surrounding hills, often laden with a light mist, on which olive and almond trees abound.

There are plenty of sights in Mallorca to satisfy the visitor in pursuit of architectural and historical delights, including the exquisite seventeenth-century Monasterio de Nuestra Señora de Lluc (*right*), just off the main highway through the north of the island. In Palma itself, the great Gothic construction of La Seu cathedral (*below*) is a dominant presence. Its near neighbour, the Palau de l'Almudaina, is an ancient Moorish fortress, later converted into a royal residence, a distinction which has now been restored to it.

mallorca **spanish islands**

Although tourism dominates the island economy, the traditional activities of the villages have proved remarkably resilient. At Cala Figuera, on Mallorca's south-east coast (*left*), there is still a great sense of pride in the local fishing community. At Porto Colom (*below*), also on the east coast, typical Mallorcan small fishing vessels lie at their moorings in front of brightly painted boat-houses.

mallorca **spanish islands**

Mallorca's western coastline, the so-called Costa Rocosa, is among the most spectacular of the whole island. Here, at Banyalbufar (*above*), dramatic cliff formations are crowned by lush vegetation. Northwards, the culmination of the coastline is a series of rocky promontories, notably the Cabo Catalunya and the Cabo de Formentor (*opposite*), where the cliff walls plunge directly into the sea.

# france

## porquerolles

The village which bears the same name as the island is a beguiling collection of fishermens' houses, residential villas and hotels, all grouped around a busy little harbour.

# porquerolles

In the midst of the frenetic hedonism of the Riviera, or lost in some beguiling village of the Provençal hinterland, it is sometimes easy to forget the chain of delightful islands which lies just twenty minutes away by ferry from the harbour at La Tour Fondue. It takes just that extra bit of effort, imagination and expense to leave the mainland, especially if you have just driven half-way across Europe. The islands, the Îles d'Hyères (also known as the Îles d'Or), once reached, are a surprising haven of calm, very different from the vibrant activity just across the water; indeed, it sometimes seems that the French, perhaps justifiably, have endeavoured to keep them something of a secret for themselves.

Porquerolles is the main island of the group and also the westernmost. Its only real community is the eponymous village which surrounds the port, spreading around the central church in a fashion peculiarly reminiscent of the small French colonial towns of north Africa. The place exudes a sense of peace, safety and goodwill; civic pride is evident everywhere you look, from the lack of litter to the obvious enthusiasm for this immaculate island on the part of its hoteliers and restaurateurs. Each evening during the summer, there is a unique 'children's market' on the square, where children buy and sell handmade arts and crafts. Unsurprisingly, the island is also a magnet for yachtsmen, and the harbour is still brimming with smart craft well outside the summer season.

Now a national park, Porquerolles offers an extraordinary array of attractions. The fact that visitors are not allowed to use motor vehicles means there are wonderful opportunities for walking and cycling. Soft, sandy beaches – notably those of Notre-Dame and the Plage d'Argent – are everything beach-lovers could wish for. Even surfing is possible when the wind rises. Bathing in the sheltered waters of the bay of Notre-Dame can only be described as luxurious, while snorkelling around its defining peninsulas introduces you to a pristine underwater environment; a litter of shipwrecks offshore provides a distinctive focus for divers. Pleasure craft compete to weigh anchor in the bay's prime positions to obtain the best diving. A number of more secluded creeks attract the adventurous; this really is a marine theme park, with the advantage of being wonderfully natural.

The waters around Porquerolles have a wonderful turquoise translucency, especially those of the bay of Notre-Dame (*opposite* and *above*), much favoured by local yachtsmen and also the location of one of the island's finest beaches.

Inland, a botanical treat lies in store for those who venture from the port and its neighbouring beaches. In addition to a profusion of wild plants, mulberries, almonds, figs, olives and peaches are all cultivated. A visit to the botanical conservatory is obligatory. Birdwatchers can expect to spot up to 163 different species. Sweeping vineyards of Côtes de Provence lie on hillsides amid unspoiled woodland, traversed by pathways. As these reach higher ground, magnificent vistas of the interior open up, revealing the lighthouse and forts rising above a carpet of treetops.

The greatest delight on this island, however, surely comes at dusk. Whether you have spent the long hours of sunshine in the sea, on the beach, or inland, there are few better ways of ending the day than dining alfresco in the village square, surrounded by trees dappled with the light of the setting sun. The local cuisine – including its plentiful seafood dishes – provides immeasurable pleasures, and then there is the absence of traffic and crowds, engendering a stress-free environment where everything seems effortless yet sumptuous at the same time.

Originally constructed by the military in the middle of the nineteenth century, Porquerolles village is arranged around its main square (*opposite*), bordered by its post-office and a modest church. Its streets are pleasantly lined with stylish cafés, restaurant and small hotels, where dining alfresco (*above*) is the norm during the summer. And even during the high season the pace of life outside seems much less frenetic than that of the Riviera resorts across the water. In part, this is due to the lack of traffic, but there is in any case a generally friendly and relaxed air about the island.

The harbour of Porquerolles (*above*), crowded with fishing and pleasure craft, is fifteen minutes by ferry from the closest point of the mainland.

The sight of bougainvillea and bicycles (*left* and *below*) in the same street seems an appropriate summing-up of the whole atmosphere of Porquerolles. Although modern property development has taken place, the islanders have in general been able to hold off the massive growth of concrete which has engulfed much of the Riviera.

Porquerolles is essentially about the quiet enjoyment of the good things
of life and of the unique ability of the French to combine successfully
simplicity with sophistication. Bars and restaurants on Porquerolles
(*above*) have an appropriately relaxed way of going about things.

Among the most favoured eating and meeting places are the Yacht Club of Porquerolles and the Club L'Escale.

41

# bay of naples and pontine islands

capri

ischia

procida

ponza

Unlike its near, larger neighbours, Ischia and Capri, Procida has never suffered from massive tourist development. The beautiful, coloured houses of its main port make it the quintessential Italian island.

# capri

There is an almost architectural majesty about the island of Capri as it soars from the turquoise, azure and aquamarine waters that lap around its encircling limestone reefs. And such is the perfection of its setting that any indulgence in water-sports there seems almost an act of irreverence. The awe-inspiring display of fluted limestone cliffs, complete with grottoes, pinnacles and arches does leave many visitors to Capri with the impression that this is indeed the most beautiful island in the whole of the Mediterranean – an opinion with which most of its inhabitants would readily concur. More circumspect travellers may argue that the immense popularity of the island makes it a

place to avoid, but its great beauty far transcends any inconvenience caused by tourist crowds. The climate and landscape are simply sublime, and there are still many unspoiled places of interest within walking distance of the main town should the human frenzy there prove too irksome.

Geographically, the compact island forms the western extremity of the dolomitic mountain chain of the Sorrentine peninsula; in Palaeolithic times it was still connected to the mainland, from which it is now separated by the Bay of Naples.

Archaeological finds have inspired the popular theory that the Greek word *kapros* (wild boar) is the origin of the island's name. Another suggests that it is derived from the Latin *capra*, meaning 'goat', arguing that the rocky profile of the island resembles the animal which later came to populate it in large numbers. However, it was not until the Romans came and bestowed their favours upon the place that the word 'Capri' acquired the exciting resonances that it holds to this day.

The island had proved irresistible to Caesar Augustus, who much preferred it to the larger, wealthier Ischia on the other side of the bay. After their arrival there in 29 B.C., the Romans developed a passion for Capri which culminated in the Emperor Tiberius building twelve villas around the island, each dedicated to a single deity on Olympus. He ruled – or mismanaged – the Roman Empire from the magnificent Villa Jovis, which today lies in ruins. The Roman occupation was followed by a long succession of rulers: the Neapolitans, the Saracens, the Normans, the Angevins and the Aragonese, before it passed into the hands of the Spanish, under whom a series of exquisite churches and convents were built in Capri and Anacapri. Early Renaissance

The visitor from the mainland will almost certainly come ashore at Marina Grande on the north coast of the island (*opposite*), the port for all the ferry and hydrofoil services. It also provides a first taste of Capri's rocky coastline, at various places off which lie the most extraordinary formations of *faraglioni* rocks (*above*).

churches were transformed by the addition of exquisite Baroque exteriors. More investment in the churches and in the island's architectural heritage followed under the Spaniards' Bourbon successors to give the towns the appearance which we still know.

The allure of Capri has remained undiluted over the centuries, developing into arguably the most fashionable retreat in the Mediterranean. It continues to draw the wealthy, and their attendant paparazzi; in fact, the name of the island has become synonymous with stylish chic. Yet, somewhere between the cliff-tops and neoclassical villas, local people are picking olives not very far away. The discovery of the Blue Grotto in the nineteenth century enormously enhanced the island's reputation; ever since it has been a favourite watering place for painters, writers, actors, exiles and eccentrics who have found themselves utterly beguiled by its beauty. And if you want to sample that special quality, just take the chairlift to Monte Solaro and look down on the wonder that is Capri.

From astounding natural scenery to urban sophistication, Capri has it all. Early evening brings the cafés in the Piazza Umberto I to life (*opposite*).

The exclusive shops of the smart streets of Capri town cater for successive waves of hedonists at the height of the summer season, from June to September (*right* and *below*).

For some of the finest views of the island, the visitor can do little better than take the chairlift from the Piazza Vittoria in Anacapri to the summit of Monte Solaro, the highest point on the island. Another location any tourist will inevitably become acquainted with is the Blue Grotto (*below*), the most famous sight on Capri and the original inspiration for the foreign tourist invasion of the island.

The views around Capri are often quite breathtaking, especially when they include architectural features. The Villa Fersen (*opposite*), south of Capri town, was used by the Versace family for parties and photoshoots; it gives magnificent views to the south-east.

One of the most famous villas on the island is that of San Michele in Anacapri (*above*), once the home of Axel Munthe (1857–1949), the Swedish physician-author and philanthropist; it now houses a display of Munthe's collection of local artifacts. Monte Solaro, reached by the chairlift from Anacapri, also yields stunning views in which the human intervention seems exactly right (*right*).

# ischia

Present-day Ischia provides something for just about everyone. The deeply furrowed flanks of centrally located volcanic Monte Epomeo, as well as being home to extensive vineyards, are forested with pine trees, ideal country for those seeking a leisurely hiking holiday. And thermal springs are never far away for those who may require rejuvenation. Around the rocky stretches of the coast, diving and yachting conditions are largely excellent and attract enthusiasts from all over Italy and beyond. Unlike Ischia's more renowned neighbour, Capri, the island does possess some excellent, long beaches, where it is often possible to see the clear evidence of a volcanic past.

Socially, Ischia is less pretentious and less exclusive than Capri, although Ischia Porto and Casamicciola have their fair share of reasonably grand hotels, thermal establishments, and a wealth of restaurants renowned for the seafood specialities created from the catches of the local fishing fleets. For the culturally-minded, the second town of Forio is an architectural gem, with a wealth of beautifully preserved Renaissance buildings. Here, narrow alleys and lanes connect a fascinating community of white-washed homes, imposing civic buildings and fine classical churches. Close to Forio are the gardens of La Mortella, laid out by Russell Page on the estate of the composer William Walton, filled with exotic species and the setting for weekend concerts by young musicians.

Given the peaceful nature of many of Ischia's pleasures, it is sometimes hard to recall that the history of this island, lying sweetly at the northern edge of Naples' majestic bay, has been much shaped by natural catastrophe and human aggression. At Ischia's heart the steep profile of Monte Epomeo remains as a constant reminder of the forces which have sometimes showered disaster on this land and its inhabitants; one eruption, in 1301, literally drowned large numbers of islanders in a sea of lava and mud. Certainly, the Romans regarded the island with some circumspection, in spite of their love of thermal baths and springs, preferring to hand it over to the Neapolitans during the reign of Augustus in exchange for the less volatile Capri, in spite of the latter being a fifth of the size of Ischia.

After the Romans, the island underwent the same barbarian invasions as nearby Capri and Procida. Then followed Germanic tribes, Saracens and Neapolitans, before the Normans established

Close to the Castello Aragonese on its rugged outcrop, Ischia presents its pleasantly aged façades to the visitor arriving from Naples. Also fascinating are the buildings of Forio, which include the exquisite

Santuario della Madonna del Soccorso, to which this row of crosses leads (*above*).

themselves there, only to see much of their achievement destroyed by a massive earthquake in 1228. Subsequently, the island was fought over by Sicilians, Turks and the Angevins of Naples.

Approaching Ischia from Naples, the boat is confronted by the formidable Castello Aragonese, one of the Mediterranean's most spectacular sights and the island's defining architectural symbol. Built piecemeal and modified over several centuries, it rises up from a cliff-edged islet just off Ischia's south-east coast and is linked to the mainland at Ischia Ponte by a narrow causeway built in 1441 by Alfonso of Aragon (hence, 'ponte'). The poetess Vittoria Colonna, friend of Michelangelo and Castiglione, lived there in the sixteenth century. Eventually, the Aragonese ceded control of the island to the French, who themselves were constantly under attack by the English fleet during the Napoleonic Wars. These successive and varied interventions in Ischia's fate have conspired, however, to create an amazingly rich cultural mix – one to go with the natural forces which have forged such a dramatic landscape and coastline.

The shops of Forio – a renowned herbalist's (*opposite*) and the Piccolo Paradiso delicatessen (*below*) – give some indication of the town's growing prosperity as *the* fashionable resort on the west of the island. Its pretty streets have also traditionally attracted artists, writers and musicians, notably the English composer William Walton.

Ischia Porto (*left*) is full of Mediterranean vigour, although the need to meet tourist demands is now making its mark. Attached to the mainland by its 1441 causeway, Ischia Ponte (*overleaf*) was once an independent fishing village topped by the Castello Aragonese, which now shelters a hotel within its walls.

# procida

Lying close to Ischia in the northern waters of the Bay of Naples, the small island of Procida is in fact the ruin of a prehistoric volcanic crater; its coastline of tufa cliffs is still crumbling slowly into the sea below. In the north-east of the island is the main settlement, built within what was the original crater. It embraces the wonderfully colourful and vibrant fishing port of Corricella, made famous as the marvellously dilapidated yet fabulously attractive background to some of the most poignant scenes in Massimo Troisi's film, *Il Postino*.

Indeed, the pastel-shaded vernacular architecture of this fishing community is almost emblematic of the island's innermost identity. Reflecting local pride, individuals often adopt different yet complementary pigments to their neighbour – often the only way of distinguishing one house from another, as shared passageways and an almost organic building style fuse Procida's habitations into a kind of communal collective.

The use of paint on the outside of its homes will inevitably reveal the origins of any Italian island. Sedimentary islands, such as Capri, are characterized by whitewashed buildings – like those in the Greek Cyclades – while the houses of volcanic islands are painted in a variety of colours, derived from the mixing of local natural materials. The friable tufa rock, for instance, occurs in an array of colours from yellow and red to brown and grey. In its geometric form, though, Procida's architecture can be traced back to Greece; any criticism that its charming townscapes have been compromised by industrial building methods will be immediately dispelled by the kaleidoscope that is Corricella's waterfront.

If the intimacy of Procida's fishing community is reflected outwardly in its architecture, its inner spirit is much informed by deeply held Catholic beliefs and traditions, and *madonnine* are to be found throughout the maze of Corricella. With the spring comes a host of church processions, the most spectacular on Good Friday and on the day dedicated to St. Michael, the patron saint of the island. The relationship with the sea and all that it provides is felt intensely on Procida. Around the bustling harbour feelings are fervently expressed, accompanied by finely orchestrated arm-waving, until a consensus brings silence and the participants in what has appeared to be fierce argument return to their houses or to the boatyards, or into a café for an eye-opening espresso and perhaps another 'discussion'.

Grouped around the harbour within the main settlement of Procida, lies the enchanting fishing village of Corricella. Much admired by film-makers for its picturesque waterfront houses (*opposite* and *above*), it is among the most photogenic of all Italian island towns.

The air of the island's tiny interior is scented by orange and lemon groves, a welcome contrast to the treeless villages. But even apparently rural roads are lined by walled farmsteads and other residences, so you are never entirely sure whether you have left one fishing community before you find you are entering another. But make no mistake, the intense intimacies of Procida certainly repay every effort to get to know them.

In spite of Corricella's fame as the archetypal Mediterranean fishing village, complete with fading façades in a multitude of hues, Procida's main town has remained relatively untouched by the tourists' enthusiasm for neighbouring Capri and Ischia. The pace of life along the waterfront is relaxed among the many inhabitants who still earn a living from the sea (*opposite* and *above*).

The organic vernacular building style of the island sometimes makes it hard to distinguish one house from another. Yet the whole place seems to thrive on its architectural chaos, the parts of which are connected by steep stone staircases. Often the only way to identify dwellings is by their colour, which often seems to complement those of their neighbours.

# ponza

Lying some 75 kilometres west of Naples, Ponza is the most spectacular of the Pontine Islands, a natural fortress rising steeply out of the tumultuous Tyrrhenian Sea. The appearance of the high, defensive cliffs of its coastline belies a gently rolling interior, much of which is given over to the cultivation of vines. But the first appearances really are quite dramatic: contorted formations of faulted and folded sediments reveal varieties of colour, reflecting their bristling mineral content. These pinnacles, spurs and caves interact with powerful gusting winds, whipping up a briny spray from the vapourizing surf, which is drawn up to hang all over the island. Fugitive rainbows appear here and there as the sun's rays catch the myriad tiny droplets.

Whether you arrive by hydrofoil or by the more leisurely ferry from Rome or Naples, the first sight of the island's port is reassuring and welcoming, a gem of eighteenth-century architectural planning. Pastel shades of yellow, pink, pale orange and blue illuminate the elegant two-tiered parade which curves neatly around the harbour's edge. There is a protective quality about the place, cosily laid out like an amphitheatre, presumably as a defence against the powerful winds which can beset the island. Tucked inside are terraced bars and seafood restaurants, offering a spectacular local cuisine. There is overall a certain air of self-importance on Ponza, from the dome of Santa Maria, the town's Renaissance masterpiece, to the neoclassical villas which seemingly jostle for position around it, to the summer homes of some of Italy's wealthier escapists.

There isn't really much in the way of island history before the eighteenth century. The Phoenicians are thought to have used the harbour as a staging-post, before the Romans established a small presence there in the 4th century B.C., but left only a few scattered remains of villas behind them. The violent cycles of raiding and pillaging which constituted much of medieval life in the Mediterranean did not spare Ponza, although it suffered much less than islands further south, like Ischia. In 1710, the island became part of the Austrian Empire and was finally ceded to the Bourbons of Naples in 1815. Mussolini was held briefly on Ponza in 1943, after the German garrison had been ousted by Allied troops.

If the notable facts of its history are relatively sparse, Ponza is certainly rich in legendary and religious associations, as any circumnavigation of the island (a real challenge by sailboat) will

Although it is still very much a working fishing port, the harbour of Ponza (*opposite* and *above*) presents the incoming visitor with a dignified array of surrounding buildings, notably the domed neoclassical church of Santa Maria.

demonstrate: the cliffs of the Madonna, the cave of Ulysses and the caves of Pilate, where Pontius Pilate is said to have reeled in catches of moray eels, a delicacy highly prized by the occupying Romans. Heading south around the Punta del Papa (named after Pope Silverio, the patron saint of Ponza, who was exiled and died there in A.D. 537), the coast becomes impossibly craggy and inaccessible to all but the bright yellow *ginestra* flowers which grow in abundance all over the island. Around this coast the sea has taken giant-sized bites out of what must have been a much more sizeable island mass, creating coves and bays which are sometimes barely separated from each other by Ponza's central spine. In one such bay lies the island's most famous tourist attraction – the fabulous beach of Chiaia di Luna, in itself a convincing enough reason for visiting Ponza.

Built in the eighteenth century, the harbour curves round to the church
of Santa Maria, which rises grandly at one end of the encircling
esplanade (*opposite*). This latter is extraordinary in that it consists of two
separate parades of buildings, the upper one stepped back from the
lower (*above*). And everywhere there are the pastel colours of another
quintessential Mediterreanean island.

This modernist interpretation of a traditional Mediterranean cuboid house looks out towards uninhabited Palmarola. The setting of the house is dramatic indeed, while the offshore island offers some of the most spectacular groups of *faraglioni* formations of any Italian island, including the massive Faraglione di Mezzogiorno.

As if its beguiling town and dramatic scenery were not enough, Ponza also possesses one of the truly great Mediterranean beaches, the Chiaia di Luna. Located on the other side of the island's spine from the main settlement, the beach is reached by a tunnel from the town side, originally constructed by the Romans. Emergence from the tunnel is an awesome experience: a shimmering beach surrounded by towering cliffs of limestone, glinting in the sun.

# egadi and aeolian islands

marettimo

favignana

lipari

vulcano

The volcanic origins of the Aeolian Islands, off Sicily's north coast, are abundantly visible today. These dramatically coloured sulphurous deposits are the result of the fumarolic activity around the crater rim of Vulcano's principal volcano.

# marettimo

The furthest-flung of all the Egadi Islands, lying off the north-west tip of Sicily, Marettimo is in many ways the most spectacular of the whole group. Separated long ago from Sicily, the island has become a sanctuary for a breathtaking variety of flora and fauna. It is a place where a profound peace is only broken by the cries of the seagulls, the reassuring rumble of the breakers and the rustling of the pine forests. There are no roads here – only a coastal path – and no hotels, leaving the visitor to negotiate with the locals for a homestay.

The island marks pretty well the exact centre of the Mediterranean, an hour and a half by hydrofoil from Sicily's western port of Trapani. A huddle of whitewashed cottages with their characteristic blue shutters and doors constitutes Marettimo's fishing port, the only settlement on an island otherwise entirely given over to nature. Its hardy inhabitants are a proud people with a strong sense of community. Around the old and new harbours fishermen sort their catches, carry out maintenance on their matching blue-painted boats and repair their nets. Those now prevented by age from putting out to sea while away the afternoon at cards or in animated conversation.

Leaving the old harbour, a trail leads towards the north-east corner of the island and the notorious castle Punta Troia, perched dramatically on a cliff-edged promontory. The original building was a Saracen stronghold, later further strengthened by the Normans, but it was the Spanish who built the existing castle at the turn of the seventeenth century, which then served as a prison until 1844. In contrast to the sinister past of the castle, where prisoners were systematically tortured both by the Spaniards and the Neapolitans, the countryside around has a new and unspoiled beauty, immediately conducive to a profound feeling of serenity.

The western half of Marettimo is even wilder; here, even the heather-fringed pathways of the eastern shore disappear. Protecting this wilderness provides precious employment for many of the island's younger generation, now unable to make a living from the declining fishing levels.

Beyond Punta Troia you will need to complete your travels by boat, but you will get some of the most dramatic views of the island: pine forests cascading down hillsides, only to be arrested in their descent by sheer limestone cliffs. All around

The most westerly of the Egadi Islands, Marettimo beyond its harbour is criss-crossed by trails. The most notable one leads to its south-eastern promontory, a place of fascination for botanists (*above*) and the site of the ruins of a seventeenth-century Spanish castle, later used as a prison (*opposite*).

the island coves and pinnacles have been carved out and shaped by the force of the sea, providing an unforgettable visual adventure during the three-hour boat trip around the whole island. To return to Marettimo's solitary settlement can also be a moving experience, as a gathering flock of seagulls heralds the arrival in harbour of one of the fleet of blue boats, laden with fish to land on the quay of the tiny port – another day in the life of the tightly-knit community of Marettimo.

Marettimo's harbour is still home to a small but active fishing fleet (*these pages*). There are no hotels among the square white houses which surround the modest waterfront, so visitors are obliged to find accommodation within the local community. In the quiet streets behind the harbour, each home is embellished with a ceramic tile bearing the name of the resident family (*overleaf*).

# favignana

The main town of Favignana is the most important of all the Egadi Islands. It is also the focus of the famous annual tuna slaughter, La Mattanza, the controversial yet extraordinary ritual which has conferred celebrity status on the town and on its colourful fishing communities and which attracts crowds of visitors each May. The centuries-old Mattanza is a kind of maritime equivalent of the bullfight – sacred to those who participate, but seemingly barbaric to an outsider. Late each spring, the huge deep-sea fish come to spawn in groups around the warmer waters of the Egadi. Here, the fishermen have

been preparing for weeks for the arrival of the fish, putting in place an ingenious sequence of suspended nets, ending in a 'chamber of death', from which there is no escape and where the final kill takes place. The fishermen are revered almost like matadors, and like matadors they honour and even worship their victims. Never complacent about the possibility of death, the men and their families know that the tuna kill can be a dangerous duel between clubs and spears and the unpredictable strength of the powerful fish. During the time of La Mattanza, prayers are said throughout the community and the island's churches are filled.

The Greeks called the place Aegusa; the present name seems to have been derived from that of the local Favonio wind in medieval times. The island is also sometimes called 'La Farfalla' (butterfly), a reference to the two 'wings', one mountainous and one almost perfectly flat, which divide the island into two distinct halves. The island's peak, capped by the Norman fort of Santa Caterina, overlooks the main town and, on either side, commands views over the whole island. This mountain, Il Monte, runs from the northern to the southern shore and is negotiable only via a tunnel. Its pale grey limestone is rough and friable from being lashed by the punishing wind and rains which can sometimes hit the island, causing rockfalls down Il Monte's treacherous cliffs. The colourful array of flora which clings to the mountain's seaward flanks also contributes to the crumbling of the rock, creating the impression of a spectacular, large-scale rock garden, from which debris occasionally cascades down into the sea below, a reminder to stick to the paths to the summit.

At the Cala Rossa, on the north-eastern corner of the island, a sort of giants' causeway has been created by the quarrying of tufa

The small port of Favignana, main island of the Egadi archipelago, lies in a large bay, bordered in parts by disused buildings dating from its time as a centre of the tuna industry (*above*). The great tuna cull, La Mattanza, still takes place every spring, for which these fishermen (*opposite*) are preparing.

The north-east coast of the island is deeply marked by the activity which, after tuna fishing, provided Favignana with substantial employment and income: the quarrying of tufa. The Cala Rossa, notably, provides pleasant rock bathing from a series of rectangular coves created by quarrying (*below*).

All the seaward flanks of the main mountain of the island are covered with a variety of plants, including heather and cacti (*opposite*). The overall effect is one of a gigantic rock-garden.

favignana **egadi and aeolian islands**

# lipari

The Aeolian Islands, of which Lipari is by far the most important, are effectively a Y-shaped group of ancient volcanoes, whose cones rise from the Tyrrhenian Sea in dramatic style. According to Homer, Aeolus the wind god kept various winds inside a cave on one of the islands; but, as Odysseus sailed by, one of these escaped, blowing the hero off his course. And it is true that wild and unpredictable winds can blow here at any time, though the summer heat usually brings a period of calm. Though Odysseus found conditions here particularly challenging, these waters make for marvellous sailing, with the added bonus of the myriad vistas provided by the islands themselves.

Lipari is the perfect base from which to explore the entire archipelago, whether by cruiser, fishing boat or ferry. The upper reaches of Monte Chirica, which dominates the island, also yield splendid views of all the surrounding islands, from the verdant slopes of Panarea and Stromboli to the north-east to the abruptly looming form of Salina to the north-west. Further west, it is possible to make out the shapes of Filicudi and Alicudi through the haze. You don't have to be a seasoned walker to enjoy many of these wonderful vistas, but the climb up Monte Chirea does induce a slightly alarming sense of the sheer steepness of the place.

The Greeks settled on Lipari during the sixth century B.C.; the Romans arrived three centuries later, building a settlement inside what is now the walled acropolis overlooking the town of Lipari. Although the Roman influence was never as strong here as on the islands of the Bay of Naples, they nevertheless left their imprint. During the imperial era, the islands were used as a detention area for criminals, though no doubt their main attraction for the Romans was the presence of thermal springs.

The fortified acropolis is a kind of historical anthology of the island: a second-century Roman settlement, a medieval cathedral, and a sixteenth-century Spanish fortress. The eleventh-century cathedral, dedicated to San Bartolomeo, is the centrepiece of the citadel. Rebuilt in the sixteenth century, after pirates had sacked the town, it has a spectacular Renaissance ceiling and its original vaulted cloisters, which somehow managed to survive amid the surrounding destruction.

The descent from the citadel, whether by the broad main steps or a series of tunnels, returns the visitor to the welcome

The largest and most developed of all the Aeolian Islands, Lipari is a place of extraordinary rock formations, indicative of its volcanic origins (*opposite*); in the background lies the crater of Vulcano. A boat trip around the island is the best way to appreciate the drama of the coastline and the views of the other islands, here stretching towards Panarea, with Stromboli beyond (*above*).

of contemporary Italy in the form of food shops and seafood restaurants which alternate with trendy bars along the pedestrianized Via Garibaldi. Eventually the way fans out into the harbour of Marina Corta, a delightful plaza of terraced cafés from which come the delicious aromas of Italian cooking and coffee-making. In all, this must be one of the most relaxed tourist towns in Italy, where the traffic is kept at bay and the horns remain silent. As the light fades and the wind drops, the restaurants set about lighting their table candles; it is impossible to imagine being anywhere else.

The main landing place for visitors is at the town of Lipari (*opposite below*), a lively community set around two ports: Marina Corta and Marina Lunga. The former (*opposite above* and *right*) is vibrant with restaurants and interesting small shops. In the evening, the streets of the main town are ideal for casual strolling, as the lights of its cafés and restaurants begin to illuminate the idyllic scene (*below*).

lipari **egadi and aeolian islands**

The waters off the east coast of Lipari (*opposite*) often take on intense shades of turquoise, a colour due to the presence of pumice dust in the water. A local industry now in decline, the quarrying of pumice causes the dust to accumulate along the shoreline and, from the so-called 'white beaches', to enter the water. Phantasmagoric rock formations alternate with the stretches of brilliant sand.

Lanes and footpaths across the island's interior make Lipari a delight for the leisurely tourist (*left above*). There are areas of gentle lowland where the visitor may come upon small communities or the occasional sanctuary. This scene near the famous viewpoint of Quattrochi (*left below*), on the west coast, shows the richness of the island's flora. Quattrochi also offers superb views of the whole island group, including the craters of Vulcano.

# vulcano

Ethereal and sometimes menacing, Vulcano is formed from four volcanoes, each the legacy of a violent phreatic eruption. This is the southernmost part of the Aeolian archipelago and its most recent addition. The dominant crater, the Vulcano della Fossa, is capped with pumice on which no vegetation can grow. Sulphurous fumaroles are still active around its rim, giving out noxious fumes and yellow sulphur. It is small wonder that Homer described the island as the workshop of Hephaestus, god of fire, as one takes in the massively striated surface of the rather menacing central core, seemingly full of destructive potential. Walkers making the tour of the crater rapidly become dwarfed by the precipitous walls of the volcano. Those who venture down inside the crater shrink to the size of ants. The height of the volcano, though, does permit the most incredible views, especially southwards over the Tyrrhenian Sea to the awesome summit of Etna. A more recent crater, Vulcanello, occupies a promontory to the north-east of the island; created about the time of Christ, its continuous fumarole activity fills the air with foul sulphurous fumes and a sinister hissing.

The remainder of Vulcano maintains a respectful distance from the central cone, and the single road on the island runs around the rim of a previous crater. It passes through files of eucalyptus, peaceful olive groves and the odd vineyard, before reaching the island's southern shore, via a series of switchbacks. Eventually, the Faro Nuovo (new lighthouse) – no longer very new – rears up above the tall sedges that skirt the pebbled shoreline.

An isolated fishing community, close to the lighthouse, supports a single, anonymous seafood restaurant. In spite of its remoteness, however, it clearly has a reputation which extends for miles. Customers seem to appear from nowhere, leaving their launches at the humble jetty. The island's main landing place is at Porto di Levante in the north, the only settlement of any significance and also the ferry port. It supports a string of cafés, sea-food restaurants and fashionable boutiques. The lack of development beyond the port has allowed Vulcano to retain a charmingly unspoiled atmosphere, born partly of a recognition of the violent powers of nature.

The upper slopes of Vulcano's main crater, the Vulcano della Fossa (*opposite* and *above*), are covered with the lava from bygone eruptions and spills and are thus devoid of any vegetation. Continuing volcanic activity in the form of fumaroles and sulphurous deposits has created a landscape in parts of red and yellow ochres. Vulcano is not conventionally beautiful, but it is certainly unforgettable.

Seen from a cliff-top on neighbouring Lipari, the volcanic form of Vulcano
is obvious (*opposite*), its formation due to the joining of four volcanoes.
On its north side is the relatively small Vulcanello, which erupted in the
latter part of the B.C. period to create its own little peninsula. The main
town of the island lies to its north, leaving the south a relatively
unspoiled place (*above*) of one or two isolated fishing communities.

For the visitor seeking the peaceful side of the Aeolian Islands, there is no better place than the southern shores of Vulcano (*these pages*). The views are spectacular, from the main crater capped by the lava above the tree-line to the distant sight of Sicily. There are very few dwellings in the area. apart from around the now no-longer new Faro Nuovo. And behind the pebbled shoreline the single road winds through groves of eucalyptus and olive trees, punctuated by the occasional vineyard.

# islands of the istrian and dalmatian coast

brijuni

dugi otok

hvar

vis

korcula

The numerous bays around Dugi Otok, like these calm waters by Luka village, make it an attractive destination for Adriatic yachtsmen.

# brijuni

From the air, just off Istria's coast, the Brijuni Islands appear as a velvet-green cluster, rimmed with golden sands and set in shallow, clear turquoise waters. Verdant forests thrive there in the absence of very much human activity, and their shores have become havens to many varieties of marine life. You can only visit Veli Brijun, the largest of the fourteen islands, as a pedestrian. From the moment the visitor sets foot ashore, it is abundantly clear that the spirit of the place is one of gentle relaxation. Go there prepared to unwind, because that is what will happen anyway. The slightly more energetic may contemplate doing a little fishing, or perhaps cycling, or even a round of golf, but to exert yourself is to miss the point completely.

A peculiar perfection in the balance between nature and its careful manipulation has been achieved on Veli Brijun. Its most obvious expression is in the trees of the island, marvellously protected and seemingly the true possessors of the island. In fact, the loudest noise you are likely to hear is the wind rustling in the trees. Even the minor sounds emitted by the wheels and brakes of your hired bicycle can seem a terrible intrusion along the pristine pathways of the forest. The only interruption might be an encounter with one of the deer that abound there.

In recent times, the Brijuni Islands achieved some fame as the private domain of the late President Tito. In ancient times, the Romans had also used them as a place for restful retreat, leaving a legacy of a few ruins. However, it was the Austrian industrialist, Paul Kupelweiser, who shaped the islands' élitist status when he bought them in 1893 with a view to creating a resort there to be used by the European aristocracy. He employed the Nobel scientist Robert Koch to rid the islands of malaria, by spraying the swamp areas with petroleum. Scrub gave way to beautifully landscaped parks and a golf course. Luxury villas and hotels were constructed to complete this paradise on earth. During the course of the twentieth century a veritable pantheon of celebrities graced the shores of the main island: Archduke Ferdinand, Kaiser Wilhelm II, Thomas Mann and James Joyce before the First World War; later visitors included Ho Chi Minh, Queen Elizabeth II, Richard Burton and Elizabeth Taylor. Their years of seclusion have left the islands looking spectacularly well, thanks to Tito's penchant for privacy and celebrity visitors.

Public access to the islands was only granted in recent years, and even today there are still cordoned-off areas reserved for the

Famous as the private retreat of President Tito and now a national park, the islands were finally opened to visitors in 1983. Among the reminders of the Tito era are the restored turn-of-the-century guest-houses that

were taken over to lodge high-profile visitors (*opposite*). Vestiges of another age include these ruins of a Roman villa on the north-eastern shore of the main island (*above*).

Croatian military. However, you may venture to the northern tip of the main island and enter a rather bizarre safari park where two elephants, given to Tito by Indira Gandhi, still mingle with zebra, camel and antelope. Another gift – four baby giraffes from Africa – were not so resilient, and now form part of the display in the permanent exhibition 'Tito on Brijuni'. Also on display is the late President's Cadillac convertible, proudly preserved as the only car on the islands.

One clear and abiding result of the special status enjoyed by Veli Brijuni under Tito is its beautifully kept and manicured appearance. The former president of Yugoslavia was, however, only continuing the work begun by the Austrian Paul Kupelweiser who, in his efforts to attract a wealthy clientele to the place, created beautifully landscaped parkland (*above*), dotted with luxury villas and hotels. All the traditional buildings like this village chapel at Luka (*opposite*), have been carefully restored and preserved. What will strike the present-day visitor is the incredible quiet, often only broken by the sound of the wind in the trees or the very faint noise emitted by a moving bicycle or electric car, the only modes of transport permitted on the island.

Brijuni has a generally rocky shoreline (*opposite*), so it will never be a great draw for beach-loving crowds. This is a place for relaxed, thoughtful vacationing, where the marvellously peaceful interior can be quietly enjoyed and punctuated with some gentle historical investigations. These can include the inspection of Byzantine ruins (*above*) or speculation about the island's rich twentieth-century social history, symbolized by the opulent Villa Brijunka, visible along the shore beyond.

# dugi otok

Stretching for over 50 kilometres, Dugi Otok is the transitional span between the green Zadar archipelago (most of the island) and the ethereal, barren landscape of the Kornats. Its name, appropriately, means 'long island': it never widens to more than 5 kilometres over its entire length, but it is the most important island along Croatia's northern Dalmatian coast. The west side is characterized by magnificent sheer cliffs of chalk; these provide a degree of protection for the leeward side of the island, where the sheltered harbours and inlets provide a pleasant environment for virtually all the settlements.

The main town is Sali, where the first records of fishing in Croatia were noted in 995. The local population (only fifteen hundred for the whole island) remains proud of this heritage and still relies heavily on the sea for its livelihood. The harbour community at Sali goes to bed early and rises early; you need to eat in good time in the evening to make sure that food is available, before allowing the tranquillity and timeless quality of the place to ensure peaceful nights. Outside Sali and one or two wine-producing hamlets you are unlikely to meet another soul. Rambles are made delightful by the fresh sea air, while

the ways through the fragrant pine woods will invariably deliver you finally to some rocky cove of unbelievably clear waters. This is a place where days can be passed in delightful, leisurely activity, which nevertheless always manages to create the appetite for that generous sea-food supper.

The peaceful, unsullied beauty of the island is a major reason why the waters around are more frequented by yachts on their way to the Kornati National Park to the south than by boats bearing terrestrial visitors. Much of the island is quite difficult of access; its spectacular cliffs are so sheer that several coastal settlements are only reachable by boat. The bay of Telascica, the island's southern natural harbour, marks the beginning of the Kornati archipelago by virtue of its relief and geology. This is one of the preferred meeting places for Adriatic yachtsmen, most of whom never bother to set foot on Dugi Otok.

It would be hard to imagine anywhere more idyllic than this island, especially for holidays where peace and quiet are the primary requirements. To call Dugi Otok 'relaxed' would be something of an understatement; although the mainland is less than 20 kilometres away, this island gem really is a world apart.

One area of attraction in this unspoiled island is the bay around the village of Luka, a place of pleasant coves (*opposite* and *above* ) and a popular destination for yachtsmen. The main part of the island has remained immune to mass-tourism; it is an excellent starting-point for exploration of the uninhabited islets of the Kornati National Park.

The political upheavals of Yugoslavia's recent past seem utterly remote from the serene, languid pace of life which is the norm here. Ferry links to the mainland coast are limited, all but disappearing in the winter months, and there is no public transport to encourage any tourist invasion.

The western, windward side of Dugi Otok is characterized by a coastline of magnificent, rugged beauty. Massive chalk cliffs (*opposite*) meet the weather fronts from the sea. This particular stretch is on the south-west tentacle of the island which stretches out towards the Kornati archipelago.

Summer does bring a multitude of small pleasure craft to Telascica (*right*). And Sali itself, the capital and largest community, possesses a busy harbour, home to a very active fishing fleet. Large excursion boats also make Telascica an important port of call on their routes during the high season.

# hvar

Nudging up against the Dalmatian coast, Hvar rises from the Adriatic as a verdant, lanceolate ridge. Its finely preserved capital, also called Hvar, is elegant and stylish – indeed, one of the most fashionable resorts of the whole Adriatic. Blessed with soothing, fragrant air, a mild climate and plenty of sunshine, the island is so agreeable that local hoteliers are said to offer money-back guarantees to guests should temperatures fall below zero in winter or the sun, which averages almost 2,800 hours a year, fail to appear during their visit. Enough rain does fall, however, to maintain a very green landscape, punctuated with fields of lavender, rosemary, sage and thyme, as well as olive groves and vineyards.

Originally occupied by Greeks from Paros in the fourth century B.C., Hvar later became part of the Roman Empire and then of that of Byzantium. In the eighth century a marauding Croatian tribe gave it its present name. The desirability of the place did not escape the notice of the Venetians, who established themselves on the island in the fifteenth century, during their drive to colonize the Adriatic. So began three centuries of sophisticated cultural and architectural achievement, expressed in the elegant layout of convents, palaces, churches and grand merchants' houses arranged artfully between Hvar's harbour and its sheltering cliff. A citadel, with commanding views over the harbour, was built above the town for its defence; the population was forced to seek refuge there when the island was attacked in 1571 by the corsair Uluz Ali.

The crenellated walls of the fortifications remain clearly visible today, tumbling down an agave-covered hillside to meet the terracotta roofs of the town. Beyond these, a neat, balustraded inner harbour, known as the Mandrac, meets the elongated main square, providing Hvar with an elegant focal point at which its vertical and horizontal dimensions are beautifully united. Its attraction to visiting yachts is obvious, the perfect place to go ashore for an evening of cocktails and elegant dining. A pleasing, pale sandstone paves the square, as well as providing the facing for St. Stephen's cathedral and the Venetian Arsenal (in which the upper storey was converted into a theatre in 1612) which dominate it. In fact, every significant building in this picturesque little harbour shares the same soft, sandy tone, giving the whole ensemble a magical, golden glow in the

The old town of Hvar (*opposite* and *above*) is the most sophisticated and elegant island capital of the whole Adriatic. Overlooked by its Venetian citadel and its defensive walls, the vibrantly busy harbour is surrounded by warm stone buildings and winding streets.

late-afternoon sun. The evening promenade, a veritable institution, brings the whole place alive at dusk, creating a chic, stylish aura reminiscent of towns along the French Riviera.

Outside the town of Hvar, the island's single road snakes around a rocky coastline of narrow inlets and ridges, tunnels through the island's steep central spine to emerge on its northern flank. Here is Starigrad, from where the ferry departs for the faster-paced mainland. Hvar's smaller communities have a relaxed air, especially when compared with the vibrancy of the main town. And, heading east, beyond the beautiful fishing village of Jelsa, lies rural bliss: lavender fields making a purple haze amid gently rolling farmland.

The main square of Hvar town, the Trg svetog Stjepana (*opposite*), runs down to join the inner harbour; its eastern end is dominated by the façade and bell-tower of St. Stephen's cathedral. Built in the sixteenth century, the campanile is distinctly Venetian in style, whereby the number of apertures increases storey by storey up to the top.

Another campanile looks over Hvar's walled harbour (*right*), where stalls selling the island's speciality crop, lavender, and other herbs and scents line the attractive quayside.

To the south of Hvar's main ferry port lies the Franciscan monastery (*above*), a foundation dating from 1461, the gift of a Venetian ship's captain, grateful for having escaped shipwreck with his life. An elaborate campanile looks down on a simple but pleasing monastic church. Further north, one of the hubs of the old town is the walled inner harbour, the Mandrac (*opposite*), where smaller boats are moored. Behind it, the main square runs up to the cathedral to create the main intersection of the town.

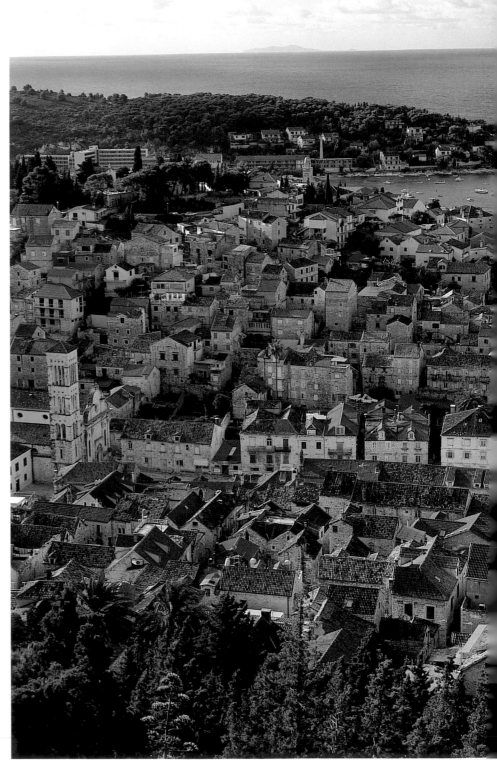

Beyond the honey-coloured buildings of Hvar's old town, the noble
campanile of the Franciscan monastery rises above the homely tiles of
the church's roof (*opposite left*). The town itself (*opposite right*) is a
confusion of lanes and houses around the main square and cathedral.
Buildings of all shapes and sizes shelter an exciting array of bars and
restaurants. Above the town the citadel sits proudly on its hill (*above*).
Part of it is now home to a marine archaeology museum; it also offers
splendid views of the town below from its defensive walls.

# vis

The tranquil air the island of Vis exudes today belies a turbulent past at the centre of many of the important naval and military engagements in the history of the Mediterranean. It is naturally defended by steep cliffs rising from the Adriatic; as the farthest offshore of Croatia's inhabited islands, it has always had a strategic importance as the guardian of the sea approaches to central Dalmatia. As such, it has had a chequered history of occupation dating back to the fourth century B.C., when it was first settled by the Greeks. The main harbour of Vis is the oldest settlement in Dalmatia, founded in 397 B.C. by Dionysus, ruler of Sicily. Little evidence remains today of the Greek occupation, save odd lumps of unadorned masonry incorporated into drystone walls.

In the wars of the nineteenth and twentieth centuries, however, Vis acquired a new significance as a central base for Mediterranean operations. After the fall of Venice in 1797, rival navies from the major European powers fought for its control. Eventually, it was seized by the British, who fortified the harbour and founded a local cricket club. They defeated a French naval force offshore in 1811. In 1815, control passed to the Austrians until the Second World War, when it was occupied by Tito's partisan forces, with British support. Tito later set up his command centre inside a cave system near the summit of Mount Hum, the island's highest point.

From the summit of the mountain an extraordinary panorama of the Adriatic opens up, from the Italian coastline in the west to the Balkan mountains in the east. Below this high point the land slopes steeply down towards the coast, but levels out sufficiently in places to provide an arable interior of rolling vineyards, flanked here and there with olive groves. The terraced vines, growing from a rich soil, produce the fine white Vugava and the red Viski wines, much prized in the region.

The main town of Vis has a stately appearance, announced by the proud and self-confident crescent of houses around the harbour. Surrounded by a cluster of cypresses, the elegant campanile of the Franciscan monastery rises above the clear blue waters of the bay, dotted with white-sailed boats which, from time to time, tack their way out towards the open sea beyond – an invitation to circumnavigation or to a landing in one of the island's secret inlets.

Vis is an island of two towns, Vis and Komiza, its main fishing port; close to the latter is a splendid fortified Benedictine monastery, seen here at sunset (*opposite*). Komiza is also the port for the small boats which take tourists to the famous Blue Grotto of Bisevo (*above*), first opened in the late nineteenth century.

At the opposite end of Vis from the main town lies the fishing community of Komiza, a place of magnificent sixteenth- and seventeenth-century Venetian houses, embellished with wrought-iron balconies, surrounding a harbour still populated with small fishing boats. Before the Second World War, the development of the fishing industry caused the population to swell considerably, but numbers later fell back during the heavy garrisoning of the island, which was only reopened to foreigners in 1989. Komiza is truly one of the gems of the Mediterranean, intimate and unspoiled, where the aroma of freshly-baked bread seems a perpetual morning presence; often flavoured with anchovies, it is the perfect accompaniment to a glass of Viski. And from the harbour you can take a boat to visit the natural wonder of neighbouring Bisevo's blue grotto. Entrance through its tiny opening can only be gained by lying flat in a small rowing boat; then there is the emergence into a vaulted cave, magically lit by shafts of sunlight which pierce through an underwater tunnel. This is one of the truly great sights of the Mediterranean and one to rival that of Capri.

The streets of Vis town (*opposite left*) curve round the bay of the harbour, viewed here from the quarter of Kut, an area of fine sixteenth-century houses (*opposite right*). One of the main features of the bay of Vis is the sixteenth-century Franciscan monastery whose campanile soars above the trees of a tiny peninsula (*below*).

Komiza, on the opposite side of the island to Vis town, is a beautifully preserved gem of a place, with a fine, tree-lined waterfront (*left*), overlooked by Venetian-style houses.

A catamaran enters the deep bay of Vis at dawn (*opposite*), with the Franciscan monastery in the background. Now a favoured destination for yachtsmen, Vis was only opened to foreigners in 1989 and has so far escaped the invasive results of mass-tourism. It has a peaceful, inviting interior (*this page*) of terraced vineyards and olive groves. The vines yield the prized reds of Viski and the whites of Vugava.

# korcula

Often referred to as 'Little Dubrovnik' because of its medieval appearance and date, the main town of Korcula is an enchanting place. Within its formidable walls, the narrow streets make an ingenious herring-bone pattern, no doubt to deflect strong winds and to keep out bright sunlight. Homes and public buildings of a warm, honey-coloured sandstone are ranged over an oval mound which protrudes into a channel separating the island from the Peljesac peninsula on the Croatian mainland. This strategic position as guardian of the channel invited century upon century of intervention by outside forces, notably the Venetians, which in turn created a rich and diverse history for the town, more than justifying the association made with its famous relative on the mainland.

The imprint of the Venetians is everywhere in the form of houses and churches. They occupied Korcula in the tenth century to bolster their ambitions in the Adriatic. It is even claimed that Marco Polo, that most famous of Venetian sailors, was born on Korcula, and a thirteenth-century house is celebrated as his actual birthplace. Though the facts are difficult to authenticate,

a climb up the outer tower of the house and the view out to sea over the terracotta roofs may well convince you that a young boy who lived there would have been inspired to become one of the greatest explorers in history. Polo certainly had a connection with the island; he was captured in a sea-battle with the Genoese there in 1298.

The main entrance to Korcula town is up an elegant nineteenth-century stairway and through the Land Gate, begun in 1391. A kind of triumphal archway was added in 1650, but after that the medieval layout reasserts itself in the form of the main artery of the town, just a few feet wide. This narrow street emerges into the irregularly shaped central square, dominated by the sheer façade of St. Mark's cathedral. Commencing in the fifteenth century, it took Korcula's skilled stonemasons one and a half centuries to complete, producing an extraordinary mixture of strangely sculpted Gothic cornices, complete with gargoyles, a sublime rose window, juxtaposed with Renaissance detailing. This architectural mix is echoed in the surrounding streets, with the further addition of seventeenth- and eighteenth-century baroque.

Under the dominating presence of its cathedral, Korcula town reveals its medieval walls and harbour (*opposite*). The narrow streets and alleyways of the old town within the walls (*above*) run right and left off the central thoroughfare.

Local legend asserts that the community of Korcula was founded by Anthenor of Troy in the twelfth century B.C. It was certainly settled by the Greeks, who named the island 'Black Corfu', after the densely wooded interior, still seen in part today. But the richest legacy really is that of the Venetians; their culture here reached its zenith between the thirteenth and fifteenth centuries, before their expansion was curtailed by the spread of plague.

Outside the main town and all around the island's coast, the land rises steeply to an interior of dark woods and open arable areas, sprinkled with lime groves. Since the break-up of the former Yugoslavia, the island has opened itself up to tourism with the provision of quite substantial hotel facilities and a yacht marina. But these really do seem like modern accretions – the true spirit of the place certainly resides within the old town walls.

One of the true treasures of the Adriatic, Korcula town presents a beguiling picture to the sea-borne visitor (*opposite*). Within the old town, narrow streets lined with venerable houses reveal themselves. There are several buildings of great beauty (*right* and *below*), including St. Mark's cathedral, one of the finest churches in the whole of Croatia.

The interior is a place of arable land, punctuated with woods and the tall forms of cypresses (*above*). A strategic strongpoint, as the guardian of the narrow channel separating the island from the Dalmatian mainland (*opposite*), Korcula town was annexed by the Venetians in the tenth century, a presence which left an indelible mark on the architecture and culture of the place.

# greek islands

corfu

zakynthos

mykonos

santorini

symi

rhodes

The postcard image of the Cyclades, Mykonos harbour is surrounded by a maze of white cuboid houses – the archetypal colours and forms of the Aegean.

# corfu

As dawn breaks over the calm waters of the narrow channel which separates Corfu's north-east coast from Albania, a succession of ships can be seen heading towards the harbour of Corfu town. The first glimpse of the island's capital from the sea reveals a place with a distinctly Venetian air; the muted pastel tones of the maritime empire's dilapidated mansions separate the grey-blue sea and sky – a pleasing composition in a real-life faded watercolour. The survivor of earthquakes and Second World War bombing, the town's exquisite Venetian heart also shows the accretions of later occupations: the British endowed it with some neoclassical additions, and the French laid the foundations of a café society. The Liston (a creation of the architect responsible for the Rue de Rivoli in Paris) fronts the green Esplanade, where the English created a cricket pitch, still in use to this day.

The narrow streets and squares which connect the elegant churches and mansions give Corfu town an air of intimacy and vibrancy. To all intents and purposes, it is the capital of the Ionian Islands; it was substantially renovated for a regional summit in 1994, and it is still looking rather spruce. The day-tripping beach tourists tend to depart in the afternoon, leaving the evenings largely to the Corfiots. After the long siesta and at the coming of dusk, the local population regains its animation; the young gossip, pose and ride their scooters; the older inhabitants converse over an aperitif at cafés along the quieter alleys and streets.

The shoreline of the island is backed by cypress-clad slopes of great scenic beauty, largely unspoiled, apart from the throbbing beach resorts that have marked Corfu indelibly on the maps of mass-tourism. Winding anti-clockwise around the northern half of the coast, skirting the mountain masses, a series of coves and promontories alternate, before the tourist strip eventually emerges near the spectacular rock formations of Peroulades. Further south, along the shore road, beautiful Angelokastro heralds the beginning of Corfu's most sumptuously endowed stretch of coast, which continues beyond the picturesque village of Paleokastritsa. This was the Homeric city of Scheria, where Odysseus was supposedly washed ashore and taken

In spite of the massive invasion of tourists and day-trippers during the summer season, there still remains a fundamental Corfu of vineyards, olive groves, churches and strong religious traditions (*opposite* and *above*).

by Nausicaa, a Phaeacian princess, to meet her father Alcinous. Along with the streets of the capital, this is quintessential Corfu: cypresses growing to epidemic levels on every jagged peninsula, cliffs plunging sheer into the Adriatic. In this context, the invasions of tourism really do seem an irrelevance, albeit a noisy one.

Approached from the sea, Corfu town reveals its Venetian ancestry (*opposite*). A place of fine buildings, like the convent on the islet of Vlahérna (*below*), just south of the main town, Corfu still has much to offer in the form of spectacular coastline and tranquil areas in its interior (*above left* and *right*).

Even though the old town of Corfu undoubtedly groans under the pressures of tourism during the summer months (*right*), the local Corfiot population still manages to go about is business of meeting in cafés for coffee and conversation (*opposite*).

The elegant neoclassicism of its villas and arcaded thoroughfares (*above* and *opposite*) gives Corfu's main town an almost Parisian feel. Indeed, the main street and its buildings were planned and constructed during the French occupation of the island.

# zakynthos

An island of contrasts and dilemmas, Zakynthos is a striking demonstration of the problems of remaining an unspoiled gem and embracing the inevitable commercialization that such raw natural beauty spawns. The 24-hour party resort of Laganas shares a bay with the endangered loggerhead sea turtles, which have been coming here to lay eggs in the soft white sand since time immemorial. Gerakas beach, on the tip of the island's southern peninsular, is one of those idyllic places that remains with you forever; the problem is that the turtles clearly feel the same way. It is here that the rival claims of tourism and environmentalism clash most violently. The National Marine Park of Zakynthos now employs volunteers from Denmark, Germany and the United Kingdom to try and keep the problem under control.

At the opposite end of the island, Shipwreck Bay draws boatloads of day-trippers to its 'inaccessible' beach. If possible, this sight – which will remain indelibly in the memory – should be visited outside the tourist season or at least at the times when the battalions of beach-lovers have departed for the day. Known locally as 'Navagio', the bay is formed at the

meeting point of two giant spurs of massive cliffs. Within, a rectangular stretch of soft white sand perfectly frames the wreck of a cargo vessel washed up there in the nineteen-sixties. The sand is churned up by incoming waves, then remains suspended in the water, creating a milky blue effect, quite surreal to the eye and in dramatic contrast to the deep blue of the sea beyond the bay. All around, the sheer, towering cliffs of dazzling white chalk present an awesome spectacle beneath their neat crown of emerald-green conifers and shrubs.

The island's namesake capital remains an attractive harbour town in spite of its post-earthquake architecture (it suffered serious damage in 1948 and again in 1953). Once known as 'the Venice of the East', the town still closely reflects the original Venetian street plan in a brave attempt to retain its integrity. Civic pride keeps the streets pristine; the evening brings them to life, with terraced cafés and restaurants providing for an all-age clientele, both tourists and islanders. *Kantadhes*, a sort of cross between Cretan folk-song and Italian opera, can be heard in the tavernas below the castle

Zakynthos is an island of breathtaking natural beauty, typified by its so-called 'Shipwreck Bay' (*opposite*). The main port remains a working fishing harbour; here, a local fisherman takes a breather after landing the morning catch (*above*).

which presides over the town. The atmosphere there is the perfect antidote to a surfeit of sun and surf. The songs, accompanied by *bazouki*, beautifully capture the spirit of the island and its people, remaining a haunting memory long after your boat has left for the mainland. This is a world away from the time-trapped villages in the mountains along the island's western flank; perhaps on no other island is the contrast so marked between those areas affected by tourism and those still leading a traditional rural life.

Away from such highly commercialized resorts as Laganas and Argassi, there are delightful stretches of coast where the good things of the island can still be enjoyed in relative tranquillity. Near the famous Blue Caves in the north of the island, a series of secluded coves offer pleasant swimming and diving conditions (*opposite*). Access to the caves themselves can be gained by boat from the little port of Ayios Nikolaos (*above*).

Rebuilt after the earthquakes of 1948 and 1953, the town of Zakynthos still conforms to its original street plan. A promenade, lined with cafés and restaurants, runs along its animated harbour (*above*). Although it is the main town, Zakynthos is not the main tourist resort and has therefore managed to maintain the distinctive identity of a working port. And for the visitor for whom the animation of this town is still too much, peaceful reflection may be inspired by monasteries inland, like Ayios Georgiou (*opposite above*) and Anafonitria (*opposite below*), both close to Shipwreck Bay.

# mykonos

Mykonos is the definitive Greek island, and one of the most familiar; its functional vernacular architecture expresses the very essence of 'Greekness'. The whitewashed, cuboid houses, embellished with their characteristic shutters, echo the colours of the national flag – an arrangement of blue and white, punctuated by the splashes of red which are the geraniums, as often as not potted in olive-oil cans.

Inside its medieval fortifications, Mykonos town is a veritable labyrinth. Whether built to conserve space within its natural lines of defence, or to protect the inhabitants from the fierce summer winds, the overall effect of the buildings and their layout is somehow far greater than the sum of the individual components. Attempting to memorize a path through the maze is a virtually hopeless task for anyone who does not live there regularly. But perhaps that was the original idea: to confuse and disorientate hostile outsiders. Today, getting lost is half the fun, and there is still that feeling of astonishment when you realize just how small the place really is. The outer reaches of the town, along its shores, are defined by some of the island's more familiar imagery: the spectacular

captains' houses, battered by the sea; the file of thatched windmills (used to process corn harvested from the surrounding islands) that stand along the ridge of Kato Myli, motionless and timeless.

Compared to many of the Cyclades, Mykonos enjoyed a pretty quiet time during antiquity. It began to flourish as a trading port in the early nineteenth century; indeed, the captains' houses were designed to store smuggled cargo. Its fame as a tourist destination, however, is of relatively recent date; the arid, hilly interior had little to entice visitors but the impressive array of beaches did, as the age of sun-worship arrived. Today, the crowds at Paradise Beach reflect Mykonos's rise in popularity: 800,000 visitors at the last annual count.

The bright, vigorous nightlife of Mykonos town exerts a powerful pull on hedonists from Sydney to New York (via Athens). As an alternative to big-city life, it has much to offer. Its present popularity began back in the nineteen-sixties, when a cosmopolitan group of artists began to come together there. Today, the town has a sophisticated air, its café-bars interspersed with designer jewelry shops and art galleries.

The famous windmills (*above*) are one of the iconic sights of Mykonos, the most popular of all the Cyclades with visitors from northern Europe and America. It clearly caters for the tourist clientele (*opposite*), yet the whole place does manage to hang on to its essential Greekness.

The island's popularity may have changed its destiny, yet its traditional architecture does remain a reassuring backdrop. In any case, the pelicans still waddle through the town's maze as the only creatures who look as though they know where they are going, and fishermen in blue caps still sell their catch at the harbour each dawn, even though they now have a café-society audience. This is really the secret of Mykonos' continuing appeal: in spite of the presence of its fashionable tourist trade, the island does manage to hang on to its Greekness, a strange yet convincing mixture of modern chic and deeply-felt tradition.

Mykonos town's labyrinthine streets crowd maze-like around the former fishermen's houses of the harbour (*above*). During the high season the waterfront is the scene of frenetic social activity (*opposite*), as myriads of tourists converge upon its bars, restaurants and cafés. Behind the waterfront, houses and streets combine in confusion, giving the whole place the air of having grown organically.

The houses of Mykonos sometimes look as they were built on top of each other; outside staircases lead to upper rooms (*above left* and *right*).

As well as extending living space, the staircases now facilitate letting to tourists.

The narrow streets of Mykonos, darting around the distinctive whitewashed houses, form a veritable maze in which it is only too easy for the visitor to lose all sense of direction (*opposite*). Those other instantly recognizable symbols of the island – the windmills (*below*) – really did have a practical application once, processing corn brought over from neighbouring islands.

mykonos **greek islands**

150

These Venetian-style houses were originally built along the town's waterfront to facilitate the landing of contraband cargoes directly from the sea (*above*). The shoreline of 'Little Venice' is now an area of galleries and bars (*opposite*), and one of the most fashionable districts of the town.

It is sometimes said on Mykonos that the island has a church or chapel for every day of the year. Whatever the truth of the claim, there are certainly large numbers of them, many of great beauty. The best-known is the Paraportiani church, west of the town harbour and made up of four interlocking chapels (*below*), but there are many other fascinating examples in the island's interior, like this tiny chapel near the monastery of Paleokastro (*opposite*).

# santorini

The only way to arrive on Santorini is by boat. Edging inside its flooded volcanic crater to weigh anchor, the visitor is inevitably overwhelmed by the sight of the towering striated cliffs above. The caldera of Santorini, or Thira as it is sometimes called, is possibly the most awesome feature of the whole Mediterranean, the remains of the most violent eruption in history. Around 1500 B.C., with a force approximately three times that of Krakatoa, the heart of the island was blown to pieces, sending tidal waves as far as Cadiz. It has been suggested that this cataclysm may have been the historical origin of the Biblical account of the parting of the Red Sea, as the Mediterranean drew in before unleashing the mighty wave. Homer also has Odysseus encountering 'floating islands', which may be a reference to the blocks of pumice thrown up by the eruption.

Ia, the island's second town, improbably attached to its northern extremity, is a rambling delight of whitewashed and pastel-shaded homes, shops, churches, studios, chapels, terraces and windmills. Sunsets here are legendary, the altitude somehow lending extra layers of colour to the horizon, and creating more

indelible memories of this magical island. Fira, the island capital, is also perched on the rim of the caldera; from the deck of an approaching ship both places appear oddly suspended above the sea. The tourist boom has swollen the main town, and it is difficult to see how it can expand much further. Cruise-ship passengers are a steady source of income for the capital's jewelry shops, restaurants and pool bars, but somewhere out of sight the island's rural economy struggles on.

A period of prosperity in the nineteenth century was introduced by mining on the island of the substantial deposits of pozzuolana, originally used in the construction of the Suez Canal. Employed as a reinforcing agent for cement, this substance was the most valuable of the mineral resources created by the ancient eruption. During mining, the remains of an ancient Minoan culture were discovered on the island's southern limb, where they had remained buried beneath deposits of ash for three millennia.

Outside the two main towns, Santorini's sloping west side supports some terraced agriculture, including a number of modest vineyards. In contrast to the fields of volcanic soil rise

The town of Ia at Santorini's northern tip (*opposite*) provides a welcome alternative to the tourist frenzy of the capital, Fira. Both, however, enjoy magnificent views over the island's caldera, a feature exploited to full advantage by this pool bar (*above*).

the white forms of the Orthodox chapels that dot the countryside, glistening in the bright sunlight. Their distinctive forms make them odd companions in the village of Pyrgos to a group of nineteenth-century neoclassical mansions, a legacy of the spurt of wealth created by the mining boom.

Santorini's volcano still smoulders in the form of the island of Neo Kameni at the heart of the caldera. While the main island represents the amazing legacy of one gigantic explosion, its black and barren offspring serves as a reminder of the powers of nature, albeit quiescent. To stand on the rim of the caldera is a spine-chilling experience, touched with much humility in the presence of such formations – the coloured layers of ash and lava that are Santorini.

The principal settlements of Santorini are ranged along the rim of the caldera and are therefore west-facing. This, coupled with their elevation above the water, means that sunsets viewed from them are usually quite spectacular. The Orthodox church at Firostefani enjoys a marvellous vantage point (*opposite*), while evening in Ia draws crowds of visitors just to view the effects of the sun slipping down below the horizon (*above*). The height of the caldera rim seems somehow to increase the intensity of the experience.

Dawn and evening light produces a particularly soothing atmosphere in Ia and Fira (*previous pages*). The latter (*above*) seems to have expanded as far as it can go on the rim of the caldera. Partly rebuilt after the earthquake of 1956, Fira is the main centre for day-trippers and parties of cruise-ship passengers during the summer months. Away from the crowds and the frenzy of Fira, the richness of the volcanic soil of the interior does mean the traditional rural life of the island is still vigorous (*opposite*). Several crops are grown, including vines, harvested by hand and donkey.

# symi

One of the most alluring sights of the eastern Mediterranean, Symi's elegant capital clusters around an enfolding natural harbour. Many a ship's passenger has made an unscheduled stop here, after catching an initial glimpse of its seductive appearance. The need to ship supplies from neighbouring Rhodes and the absence of anything like enough flat land to build a runway have helped to limit the tourist tide and to preserve this island's charming integrity.

The protected nineteenth-century Italianate architecture gives the harbour area of Yialos an ordered look; honey-coloured villas step up the hillside above it to blend eventually with Horio on the saddle of the hill. The elegance of the houses is testimony to the prosperity once enjoyed by Symi from the export of sponges and fine wooden ships, though the building of the latter left the island largely treeless and created its present arid, denuded appearance. The drop in demand for the ships and the loss of the sponge trade to Kalymnos eventually led this once prosperous place into economic decline. Worse followed in 1945, when German forces wrecked most of Horio by blowing up an ammunition dump and the Allies bombed Yialos, damaging many of the fine mansions and villas. Over recent years, however, both towns have been painstakingly rebuilt and restored pretty well to their original splendour. Tourists seeking respite from the crowds of Rhodes have provided the incentive for the conversion of many of the dwellings into holiday villas.

The siesta on Symi is a lengthy business and a necessary escape from the heat of the sun-baked slopes. A rocky coastline is punctuated here and there with gravel beaches which offer some alternative relaxation in the form of bathing and snorkelling. Out of season, or before the temperature rises, the interior offers some enticing walking routes crossing to the bays on the west of the island via a series of eighteenth-century monasteries. For the less energetic, excursion boats leave the quayside in Yialos every few hours for a number of landing points around the coast.

Yialos exerts an irresistible attraction for yachtsmen, especially since the neighbouring Turkish coast is a sailor's delight. And where better to make the transition to Greek waters? A decent gathering of sea-food restaurants skirts the

The fine houses around the superb natural harbour of Symi indicate that this was once a place of great prosperity (*opposite*). Above the port itself lies Horio, with fine old houses and churches along atmospheric streets (*above* and *overleaf*). There, the Hatziagapitos Mansion (*p. 165*) has been restored to serve as a local museum.

harbour, alongside a number of well-stocked supermarkets-cum-delicatessens, from which the glamorous craft in the harbour can draw suitably delectable supplies. Even the liquor is duty-free. And any camera-shy celebrity will be pretty certain to find this a paparazzi-free zone. There is a timelessness about the island and its twin towns that begins to infect the consciousness after a certain period. The hour to board the boat to depart Symi's shores is certainly not a welcome arrival. For those who stay, there is the visual joy of living in one of the prettiest small ports in the Aegean, with the assurance that its status as a conservation area will guarantee its present appearance and the survival of its elegant houses for a very, very long time.

Yialos harbour (*previous pages* and *opposite*) has a natural beauty made greater by the wealth of Italianate mansions that line the hillside above the waterfront. Many of these were damaged during the Second World War, but have now been largely restored to form part of a heritage area. As well as being a summer day-tourist centre, the harbour also attracts pleasure and fishing craft (*below*). Above, there is a steep climb via stepped paths to Horio (*left*).

# rhodes

It doesn't take long on Rhodes to recognize the reasons why it is one of the most popular islands in the Mediterrranean: a string of great beaches along the eastern shore, sumptuous landscapes, and its exquisitely preserved and enthralling medieval capital, built by the Knights of St. John. Its strategic position, just off the coast of Turkey, along with an equable climate, destined the island for importance for centuries before Christ, when the Colossus of Rhodes – one of the Seven Wonders of the Ancient World – is said to have stood at the entrance to Mandhraki harbour.

Founded in 408 B.C., the old town of Rhodes reveals its cosmopolitan origins at every turn. Along with Jerusalem and Malta's capital, Valletta, it is one of the finest surviving examples of a medieval city. The fortifications and narrow streets, with their buttressed walls, are still largely intact, made even more attractive by exquisite Ottoman features, like the Library and the Suleymaniye Mosque. The old coffee-houses around Odos Sokratous (the centre of the bazaar) create an atmosphere in the local streets more akin to that of Istanbul's Grand Bazaar than to anything Greek. Elsewhere, synagogues, neoclassical mansions and Byzantine merchants' houses stand side by side in a rich, multi-cultural mix. The whole is dominated by the Palace of the Grand Masters. Reconstructed by the Italians in 1940 after being partly destroyed by an explosion in an ammunition depot in 1856, it later became the summer residence of Mussolini and Victor Emmanuel III. Its restored exterior closely follows the original, but the interior is marred by the inclusion of the marble so beloved of Fascist architects and designers, jarring oddly with more ancient features, like the mosaics from the island of Kos.

The sweeping central and southern landscape, much planted with olive groves, has more a look of the Middle East than any of the other Greek islands. An undulating interior is flanked by mountainous coastal strips, occasionally revealing glimpses of the sapphire eastern Mediterranean between spurs of land. The windward western coast has a lusher coastal strip, at its most dramatic around Monolithos. There are, however, spectacular sights on the arid eastern coast, most famously at Lindhos, a dazzling white town built around a group of captains' houses dating from the sixteenth and seventeenth centuries. On the bluff above the town lie the remains of the ancient acropolis, strewn within the confines of the medieval castle. From there, you

The windward, west coast of Rhodes is damper and therefore more obviously wooded; this view looks out towards the islet of Alimnia (*opposite*). These columns bearing, respectively, a stag and a doe (*above*) supposedly mark the position of the feet of the ancient Colossus which stood astride the Mandhraki harbour entrance.

can gaze down on St. Paul's harbour, where the apostle is believed to have landed in A.D. 58 on his evangelical mission to the island.

Rhodes is probably one of the sunniest places in Europe, which guarantees flight after flight of holidaymakers from the greyer climes of northern Europe. Tourism is a major industry here and many of the resorts do become hopelessly overcrowded in season. Thankfully, the island capital has managed to remain aloof from the worst excesses of the visitors, but even it has been exploited for its nightlife appeal. Its magnificent architectural presence, though, always seems to rise above the clamour of its evolving popularity.

It is not hard to see why Rhodes is subject to so much tourist and commercial pressure: all parts of it, apart from the specialist holiday resorts, are so photogenic. From the walls and alleyways of its fortified medieval city (*opposite*) to its coastline and the settlements around it, the island is a visual and cultural delight. The town of Lindhos, overlooked by its citadel (*right*), remains a spectacular, must-see sight, although it is inundated with visitors during the summer. On the opposite side of the island are the old fortifications of Monolithos on a bluff overlooking the sea (*below*); a pretty chapel is contained within the old castle walls.

There are plentiful remaining signs of the Ottoman occupation of Rhodes town, which began after the expulsion of the Knights of St. John in 1522–23. These include the great Suleymaniye Mosque, a largely nineteenth-century edifice built over sixteenth-century foundations (*opposite above left*). There is also an Ottoman library near the mosque, while many streets have a distinctly Islamic look (*opposite below*). One important vestige of the Byzantine period is the monastery at Tharri, in the interior west of Lindhos (*opposite above right*). This is the oldest religious foundation on Rhodes; it contains important frescoes and was recently re-established as a working community.

In response to the popularity of the town of Rhodes as a tourist destination, there is plentiful accommodation, some of it of great distinction. The Marco Polo Mansion (*left*), for instance, is a beautifully restored and refurbished traditional Turkish house, furnished with fine antiques.

rhodes **greek islands**

# tunisia

## djerba

The beaches of Aghir, on Djerba's south-east coast, are far less subject to tourist pressures than their neighbours to the north. Here, some traditional fishing communities still flourish, as this colourful and animated scene testifies.

177

# djerba

On the tenth day of *The Odyssey*, Odysseus arrived with his fleet in waters off the coast of the country of the lotus-eaters. Three men were sent to land on a reconnaissance mission but, after encountering the inhabitants and tasting the nectar of the lotus fruit, lost all desire to return or even to communicate with their comrades. Djerba lays claim to being the original of that mythical land, perhaps more believably than Gozo or Menorca, which make similar boasts. The guaranteed sunshine, white sand and turquoise waters admittedly mark the island out as a hedonist paradise; it is also home to a uniquely cosmopolitan culture.

Unmistakably African, the island is effectively a flat segment of desert, with white sandy beaches. The longest of these, Sidi Mahrez, has spawned a highly developed *zone touristique*, where every imaginable beach activity is on offer, from windsurfing and paragliding to volleyball and soccer. It is also a good place to perfect a suntan. The presence of licensed hotel bars and even a casino announces that this is a somewhat surreal strip of Tunisia. Exquisitely maintained golf-courses skirt the tourist area, constantly watered oases in a parched landscape to maintain a strange, verdant freshness.

Away from the international tourism of Sidi Mahrez, Djerba has a rich and peculiar multi-ethnic culture, remarkably distinct from that of the Tunisian mainland, just two kilometres away. Arabs, Jews, Berbers, black Africans and Muslims of both the Sunni and Ibadite sects all share this island in, for the most part, convivial harmony. The history of the place is also a complex mix. It was settled by the Carthaginians, who sheltered their ships in the near-landlocked gulf. The Romans founded a city on the southern coast, of which there are several remains. But it was the Arab invasions and, most specifically, the growth of the ascetic Ibadite sect – known for its piety and its opposition to centralist rule by the caliphs – which contributed one of the dominant strands to present-day Djerban culture. In the south and west of the island, where Ibadite communities predominate, all business stops at prayer times and the walls of the mosques are ringed with bicycles propped against them by worshippers. The mosques themselves – like many simple dome-roofed dwellings – are constructed defensively in a manner unique to the island, a legacy of Christian raids which began in the twelfth century, notably from Sicily when that island was under the Aragonese.

The rocky west coast of Djerba has remained relatively untouched by tourism: here, a typical stretch near the fortified mosque of Sidi Yati (*opposite*). Houmt Souk, the island's capital, is full of historical sights, including the sixteenth-century fortress of Bordj el Kebir by the harbour (*above*).

About 1500 Jews live on Djerba, generally in peaceful co-existence with their Muslim neighbours. The origins of this community are obscure, but certainly of great antiquity. Their extraordinary El Ghriba ('miracle') synagogue, said to stand on the site of an original dating from 586 B.C., lies in the centre of the island and draws Jewish pilgrims from all over northern Africa on the thirty-third day after the beginning of Passover.

The island's interior is pleasantly scattered with olive and date-palm groves, interspersed with over two hundred whitewashed mosques and marabouts; there are few places where a minaret is not visible somewhere on the horizon. Djerba's real social centre is the bustling market town of Houmt Souk, on the north coast, which has grown from a small port engaged in octopus fishing. Its souk is a veritable Aladdin's Cave, still with an air of authenticity and undoubted charm in a confusion of whitewashed medieval buildings with blue-painted shutters and doors. Venture inside to discover the *zaouias* (tiled courtyards built around marabouts), caravanserais, residences and workshops, all in a delightful jumble. And if the sun gets too hot, you can indulge in the French legacy of *baguettes*, *jus d'orange* and *café au lait*.

This profusion of street signs near the Mosquée des Étrangers in Houmt Souk (*opposite*) leaves no doubt about the importance of tourism to Djerba. However, there are places in the main town where traditional café life does not seem to have been overrun by visiting crowds (*above* and *right*) and where mint tea is still drunk and games of dominoes still played.

The most important site of Djerba's long-established Jewish community is the El Ghriba synagogue. In its present form, dating from the 1920s, the shrine consists of a large tiled hall (*above left*) within a whitewashed exterior. The original synagogue was reputed to be the oldest in the Jewish world, dating from the first settlement in Djerba in 586 B.C. by Jews fleeing Jerusalem after the destruction of the temple of King Solomon. The profusion of coloured ceramics within the present

building is a reminder that Djerba has long been a centre of pottery production. The flickering oil lamps of the synagogue's interior (*above right*) shed a soft light over the tiled walls. Of great importance to Muslims in the seventeenth-century Zaouia of Sidi Brahim (*opposite*) in the centre of Houmt Souk; it shelters the saint's mausoleum and was famed as a college for religious studies.

A world away from the tourist developments of the north-east is the sparsely populated western coast, where fishing is still the staple activity. It is here that surviving examples of the classic Djerban domestic dwelling – the *menzel* – are most likely to be found (*above*).

Windowless exterior walls made it defensible, while plentiful storage rooms and a water-storage system made it self-sufficient in troubled times. One traditional Djerban habitation (*opposite*) achieved world-wide fame as Obiwan's house in the first *Star Wars* film.

Not surprisingly, given the name of the town, Houmt Souk is an important market centre, and twice a week special markets around the souk attract people from all over the island to buy spices, foodstuffs and ornamental wares (*this page*). Within the souk area, several old caravanserais have been converted into interesting small hotels. These were the hostelries in which the merchants of past times would have stayed while attending local markets. Beyond the Moorish entrances (*opposite*), rooms are arranged around an internal courtyard.

# malta
## gozo

Gozo is a diminutive gem of an island, so small that a panorama of much of its interior and many of its villages opens up from the citadel of the capital, Rabat.

# gozo

Edward Lear's oft-quoted description of Gozo's coastal scenery in 1866, as being 'pomskizillious and gromphibberous, being as no words can describe its magnificence…', indicates that this is an island of very special quality. Any visitor arriving from Malta at the charmingly chaotic little port of Mgarr on the south-east coast will be struck by the individuality of the place. Indeed, it is much that Malta is not: it has resisted the worst excesses of commercial exploitation; it is verdant and agricultural; it moves at a pace to satisfy the most leisurely of tourists.

It was this relative sleepiness, coupled with the generally relaxed (though underscored by a fierce sense of independence) lifestyle of the Gozitan community, which made the island traditionally an attractive place for discerning northern Europeans seeking second residences in the sun. Visitors to the island have not always been as welcome as those who settled or vacationed there during the past forty years. Although nominally under the protection of the Knights of Malta, Gozo's benign landscape and undefended coastline acted as magnets to marauding Turks and privateers who raided the island during the sixteenth and seventeenth centuries for slaves. In 1551 almost the entire population of the island was taken into slavery.

The violent times are past now, and once the visitor has negotiated the entirely beguiling anarchy of Mgarr port, the gentle face of Gozo begins to unveil itself. At the heart of the island lies the diminutive capital, named 'Victoria' in honour of Queen Victoria's Diamond Jubilee of 1897, but known by its traditional name of Rabat to most Gozitans. A place of elegant balconied houses grouped around a majestic citadel, Rabat enjoys energetic mornings and evenings, and somnolent afternoons. The citadel encloses some significant museums and the cathedral; it also yields quite magnificent views over the island's landscape, a scene of hills capped with very large churches surrounded by villages. These latter are varied and interesting, pronouncing the island a paradise for the reflective tourist rather than the all-action, swimming, snorkelling aficionado, who may prefer the neighbouring islet of Comino, which offers some of the finest watersport in the eastern Mediterranean.

Here, on Gozo, sights like the prehistoric 'temples' of Ggantija, thought to be among the oldest surviving monuments in the world, or the splendid village square of the old capital of Xaghra, or the overwhelming rotunda of Xewkija are to be savoured

The engaging chaos of Mgarr's harbour (*opposite*) is likely to be most people's first experience of Gozo. Around the island's coast, the clear waters make for wonderful swimming and diving – here, at Xlendi, a bay south-west of Rabat (*above*).

slowly. This latter building is outstanding even on an island where every village seems to be dominated by a large church; it has the second highest dome internally in Europe after St. Peter's in Rome, and is slightly higher externally than St. Paul's in London. If that leisurely Gozitan swim is needed after viewing the sights, there are always the red sands of Ramla Bay, close to the Homeric Calypso's Cave, allegedly the scene of the enticement of Odysseus by the nymph Calypso.

Pretty well the whole of Gozo's coastline remains wild, unpredictable and relentlessly breathtaking. That an island which measures just 14 kilometres at its widest point can contain so many fascinating natural phenomena seems improbable. Its multitude of inviting coves are a scuba diver's dream, bathed in waters of clear turquoise and azure, and brimming with life in an enthralling underwater seascape.

It is possible to walk almost anywhere on the island if you feel like it, as each community leads effortlessly towards the next. The pace of life is so unrushed that, if you do take to a car, it seems absurd to move into fourth gear, let alone fifth. By the time you have shifted up, it is time to drop down again, because by then you will have seen something to make you want to stop and get out. Everywhere, there is still the sense of traditional, laid-back charm. But plans for an international airport and other development projects could play havoc with the easy-going relationship between the growing contingent of tourist visitors and their 20,000 hosts.

Virtually every section of Gozo's varied coastline offers some form of visual or sporting excitement to the visitor, from the Azure Window at Dwejra (*opposite*), the island's western limit, to the red sandy beach at Ramla Bay, on the north coast (*left*). Also on the north coast, west of Marsalforn, the crystalline rocks around Xwieni (*below*) (which provide good swimming) have traditionally been quarried into salt-pans, yielding a coarse sea-salt, still produced today (*overleaf*).

Gozo is an island of surprises, often in the form of buildings and institutions which seem too large and important for so small a place. Xaghra, for instance, north-east of Rabat, has a fine toy museum (*left above*), the Pomskillious, named after Edward Lear's concocted adjective to describe Gozo's coastline. The village is also the base from which to explore the temples of Ggantija.

Inside Rabat itself, a good place to spend a somnolent afternoon in a café (*left centre*), the citadel on the north side of the town encompasses an amazing number of impressive buildings, all in pleasantly aged old limestone (*left below*). The original citadel was Roman, with later Arab additions; there is now a Norman area, a Baroque cathedral, a palace, and four museums: Cathedral, Folklore, Natural History and Science, Archaeological, and Old Prisons. But perhaps the most remarkable recent monument in Gozo is the towering church of St. John the Baptist (*opposite*), rising high above the village houses of Xewkija. A mid twentieth-century structure built over a seventeenth-century church, the dome's design is based on that of the Salute in Venice and rises higher than that of St. Paul's in London.

# travellers' guide

While every effort has been made to ensure that the information given in the following entries is correct, the author and the publisher cannot be held responsible for any inadvertent inaccuracies. The Travellers' Guide is not intended to be a conventional guide, but is based on the author's tastes and preferences. Conventional guidebooks should be consulted if further information is required.

## spanish islands

## ibiza

### TRANSPORTATION
BY PLANE There is a huge range of flights from Britain and northern Europe to Ibiza. Inter-island flights are scheduled by Iberia (www.iberia.com) and Air Europa (www.aireuropa.com).
BY FERRY Baleària (www.balearia.com) and Trasmediterránea (www.trasmediterranea.es) run inter-island ferries and hydrofoils as well as car ferries and catamarans to and from the Spanish mainland.
BY BOAT There are regular boat services from Ibiza Town to Es Canar, Platja d'en Bossa, Santa Eularia des Riu and Talamanca.
BY BUS There are regular bus services from Ibiza Town to Figueretes, Platja d'en Bossa, Portinatx, Sant Antoni, Ses Salines, Santa Eularia des Riu, Sant Joan, Sant Miquel, Sant Josep and the airport.

### HOTELS
HOSTAL RESIDENCIA LA VENTANA, Sa Carrossa 13; tel. +34 971 390 145.
LA TORRE DEL CANÓNIGO (fourteenth-century tower), Calle Mayor 8, Dalt Vila; tel. +39 971 303 884; www.elcanonigo.com.
HOTEL VICTORIA, Ctra. San Agustín, Cala Tarida km 3, San José; tel. +34 971 340 900; www.victoriaibiza.com.

### RESTAURANTS
LA MARINA (excellent seafood), c. Barcelona 7; tel. +34 971 310 172.
LOS PASAJEROS, c. Vicent Soler 6.
LA VICTORIA, c. Riambau 1; tel. +34 971 310 622.

### FESTIVALS
16 January, Revetla de Sant Antoni Abat (lighting of bonfires); 21 January, Festa de Santa Agnes de Corona (traditional dancing, music, fireworks); festivities throughout Ibiza in the week before Lent; 19 March, Festa de Sant Josep (live classical music and fireworks); 5 April, Festa de Sant Vicent; 23 April, Festa de Sant Jordi (donating of books and traditional dancing around the island).

### SIGHTS
Dalt Vila (Ibiza's old town); Sa Penya (old walled town and fishermen's quarter); many of Europe's top nightclubs.

## mallorca

### TRANSPORTATION
BY PLANE There is a huge range of flights from Britain and northern Europe to Mallorca. Inter-island flights are scheduled by Iberia (www.iberia.com) and Air Europa (www.aireuropa.com).
BY FERRY Baleària (www.balearia.com) and Trasmediterránea (www.trasmediterranea.es) run inter-island ferries and hydrofoils as well as car ferries and catamarans to and from the Spanish mainland.
BY BUS Regular bus services operate around the island.
BY TRAIN There are regular trains from Palma to Binissalem, Inca and Soller.

## HOTELS

HOTEL RESIDENCIA PALACIO
CA SA GALESA,
c. Miramar 8, Palma;
tel. +34 971 715 400;
www.palaciocasagalesa.com.
HOTEL SOL JAIME III,
Passeig Mallorca 14, Palma;
tel. +39 971 725 943.
HOTEL VALLDEMOSSA,
Ctra. Viejade Valldemossa, Valldemossa;
tel. +34 971 612 626;
www.valldemossahotel.com.

## RESTAURANTS

CA'N CARLOS,
c. de S'Aigua 5, off Avga,
Jaume III,
Palma;
tel. +34 971 713 869.
CELLER SA PREMSA,
Plaça bisbe Berenguer de Palou 8, Palma;
tel. +34 971 723 529.
PIPISTRELLO
(converted sixteenth-century stables),
c. Concepció 34, Palma;
tel. +34 971 715 601.

## FESTIVALS

16 January, Revetla de Sant Antoni Abat
(lighting of bonfires in Palma and several
other villages, especially Muro and Sa
Pobla, where the villagers wear fancy
dress); 17 January, Beneides de Sant Antoni
(in Sa Pobla and Arta); 19 January, Revetla
de Sant Sebastia, followed by the Festa de
Sant Sebastia on 20 January in Pollenca;
carnival throughout Mallorca in the week
before Lent; Maundy Thursday, religious
procession in Palma's streets; Good Friday
processions in Palma, Sineu and Pollenca.

## SIGHTS

Palma Cathedral; Palau de L'Almudaina;
Museu de Mallorca; Basilica de Sant
Francesc; Valldemossa and its Carthusian
monastery (Real Cartuja de Jesus de
Nazaret); Renaissance mansions of Old
Palma; Monastery of Lluc; Drac caves.

# france

## porquerolles

### TRANSPORTATION

BY PLANE  There are daily flights from
Paris to Toulon-Hyères airport.
BY CAR  From Paris, take the A7, then the
A8 towards Aix-en-Provence and then
follow the A570 as far as Hyères. Take the
D97 to La Tour Fondue (pier to
Porquerolles).
BY BOAT  TLV (www.tlv_tvm.com) and Taxi
Boat Le Pélican (www.locamarine75.com)
run regular boat services from La Tour
Fondue to Porquerolles.
BY TRAIN  There is a daily rail link from
Paris to Hyères.

### HOTELS

LE MAS DU LANGOUSTIER;
tel. +33 04 94 58 30 09.
RELAIS DE LA POSTE;
tel. +33 04 98 04 62 62;
www.lerelaisdelaposte.com.

### RESTAURANTS

RELAIS DE LA POSTE;
tel. +33 04 98 04 62 62.
YACHT CLUB PORQUEROLLES,

Hyères;
tel. +33 04 94 58 34 37.

### SIGHTS

St. Agatha's Fort (sixteenth-century);
Fort de la Repentance;  La Palud beach,
Solitude Valley; Notre-Dame bay.

# bay of naples and pontine islands

## capri

### TRANSPORTATION

BY PLANE  Both Naples harbours are
about 20-30 minutes' drive from Napoli
Capodichino airport.
BY FERRY  There are regular ferries and
hydrofoils to Capri: Alilauro
(www.alilauro.it), Caremar
(www.caremar.it), Linea Jet (www.navlib.it)
and Linee Lauro (www.lineelauro.it)
operate services from Molo Beverello dock
in Naples; Alilauro and SNAV
(www.snavali.com) operate services from
Mergellina in Naples; Linee Marittime
Partenopee and Caremar operate services
from Sorrento.
BY CAR  From Rome, take the A1 to Bari,
the A16 to Salerno and the A30, following
the road markings for the Tangenziale.
Take Exit 12 at the Via Campana and
continue towards the harbour of Pozzuoli
(ferry).  To reach the harbour of Naples
Beverello (ferry and hydrofoil), follow the
road markings for the Zona Portuale and

continue to the harbour.

BY BUS  Frequent buses run from the Marina Grande to Capri or Anacapri and the funicular runs up to Capri Town every 15 minutes between 6.30 a.m. and 12.30 a.m.  Regular bus services operate between Capri Town and Anacapri, Damecuta and Marina Piccola.

BY CHAIRLIFT  From Anacapri to Monte Solaro.

BY TRAIN  There are four railway stations close to the Naples harbours: Napoli Campi Flegrei (3 km from Mergellina); Napoli Mergellina (200 m from Mergellina); Napoli Centrale; Napoli Piazza Garibaldi (4 km from Molo Beverello).

## HOTELS

HOTEL GATTO BIANCO,
Via V. Emanuele 13;
tel. +39 081 837 5143;
www.gattobianco-capri.com.
HOTEL PUNTA TRAGARA,
Via Tragara 57;
tel. +39 081 837 0844;
www.hoteltragana.com.
HOTEL QUISISANA,
Via Camerelle 2;
tel. +39 081 837 0788;
www.quisi.it.

## RESTAURANTS

DA GELSOMINA ALL MIGLIARA,
Via La Migliara 72, Anacapri;
tel. +39 081 837 1499.
DA GEMMA,
Via Madre Serafina 6;
tel. +39 081 837 0461.
DA GIORGIO,
Via Roma 34;
tel. +39 081 837 0687.

## SIGHTS

Blue Grotto; Villa San Michele and Church of San Michele in Anacapri; chairlift to Monte Solaro.

# ischia

## TRANSPORTATION

BY PLANE  Both Naples harbours are about 20-30 minutes' drive from Napoli Capodichino airport.

BY FERRY  There are regular ferries and hydrofoils to Ischia: Alilauro (www.alilauro.it), Caremar (www.caremar.it), Linea Jet (www.navlib.it) and Linee Lauro (www.lineelauro.it) operate services from Molo Beverello dock in Naples; Alilauro and SNAV (www.snavali.com) operate services from Mergellina in Naples; there are also ferries from Pozzuoli.

BY CAR  From Rome, take the A1 to Bari, the A16 to Salerno and the A30, following the road markings for the Tangenziale. Take Exit 12 at the Via Campana and continue towards the harbour of Pozzuoli (ferry).  To reach the harbour of Naples Beverello (ferry and hydrofoil), follow the road markings for the Zona Portuale and continue to the harbour.

BY TRAIN  There are four railway stations close to the Naples harbours: Napoli Campi Flegrei (3 km from Mergellina); Napoli Mergellina (200 m from Mergellina); Napoli Centrale; Napoli Piazza Garibaldi (4 km from Molo Beverello).

## HOTELS

GRAND HOTEL EXCELSIOR,
Via Emanuele Gianturco 19;
tel. +39 081 991 522;
www.excelsiorischia.it.
GRAND HOTEL
PUNTA MOLINO TERME,
Lungomare Cristoforo Colombo 23;
tel. +39 081 991 344;
www.puntamolino.it.
HOTEL TERME SAN MONTANO,
Via Monte Vico, Lacco Ameno;
tel. +39 081 994 033.

## RESTAURANTS

CAVA DELL'ISOLA,
Via G. Mazzella 17;
tel. +39 081 997 452.
DA PASQUALE,
Via S. Angelo Coatro 79, Serrara Fontana;
tel. +39 081 904 208.
OASIS SAPORI ANTICHI,
Via Provinciale, Vallesaccard;
tel. +39 082 797 021.

## FESTIVALS

June, rally of antique cars;  4–8 August, taste wines from 30 different companies; September, Vittorio Da Sica Cinema Festival;  16–19 October, Pasta Show (celebrates art of pasta-making); October, Walnut Festival.

## SIGHTS

Ischia Ponte; Sant' Angelo; Castello d'Ischia (group of castles on tiny island near Ischia, including several churches dating from the 14th century); Monte Epomeo.

# procida

## TRANSPORTATION

BY PLANE  Both Naples harbours are

about 20-30 minutes' drive from Napoli Capodichino airport.

BY FERRY There are regular ferries and hydrofoils to Procida: Alilauro (www.alilauro.it), Caremar (www.caremar.it), Linea Jet (www.navlib.it) and Linee Lauro (www.lineelauro.it) operate services from Molo Beverello dock in Naples; Alilauro and SNAV (www.snavali.com) operate services from Mergellina in Naples; there are also ferries from Pozzuoli.

BY CAR From Rome, take the A1 to Bari, the A16 to Salerno and the A30, following the road markings for the Tangenziale. Take Exit 12 at the Via Campana and continue towards the harbour of Pozzuoli (ferry). To reach the harbour of Naples Beverello (ferry and hydrofoil), follow the road markings for the Zona Portuale and continue to the harbour.

BY BUS Regular bus services between the harbour and Chiaiolella.

BY TRAIN There are four railway stations close to the Naples harbours: Napoli Campi Flegrei (3 km from Mergellina); Napoli Mergellina (200 m from Mergellina); Napoli Centrale; Napoli Piazza Garibaldi (4 km from Molo Beverello).

## HOTELS
CRESCENZO,
Via Marina Chiaiolella 33;
tel. +39 081 896 7255.
EL DORADO,
Via V Emanuele 236, Chiaiolella;
tel. +39 081 896 8005.
RIVIERA,
Via Giovanni da Procida 36;
tel. +39 081 896 7197;
www.hotelrivieraprocida.it.

## RESTAURANTS
IL CANTINONE,
Via Roma 55;
tel. +39 081 896 8811.
CRESCENZO (good pizzeria),
Via Marina Chiaiolella 33;
tel. +39 081 896 7255.
LA MEDUSA,
Via Roma 116;
tel. +39 896 7481.

## FESTIVALS
St. Michael's Day in Spring; Holy Week processions at Easter, culminating on Good Friday.

## SIGHTS
Painted fishermen's houses and workshops of Chiaiolella; Abbey of San Michele Arcangelo; Castello d'Avalos.

# ponza

## TRANSPORTATION
BY PLANE Rome or Naples are the best starting points for travelling to Ponza.
BY FERRY Ferries and hydrofoils run to Ponza from Anzio (1 hour from Rome by train), Terracina and Formia. In summer there is an additional hydrofoil service from Ischia to Ponza (Alilauro).
BY CAR From Rome, take the A1 to Bari, the A16 to Salerno and the A30, following the road markings for the Tangenziale. Take Exit 12 at the Via Campana and continue towards the harbour of Pozzuoli (ferry). To reach the harbour of Naples Beverello (ferry and hydrofoil), follow the road markings for the Zona Portuale and continue to the harbour.

BY BUS Regular bus services between Ponza Porto and Le Forna.

## HOTELS
GRAND HOTEL CHIAIA DI LUNA,
Via Panoramica;
tel. +39 0771 80113.
HOTEL MARI,
Corso Pisacane 19;
tel. +39 0771 80101;
www.hotelmari.com.

## RESTAURANTS
AFFITACAMERE RISTORANTE ARCOBALENO,
Via Scotti di Basso 6;
tel. +39 0771 80315.
HOTEL GENNARINO A MARE,
Via Dante 64;
tel. +39 0771 80071.
RISTORANTE LA PALMA,
Via Loggia S. Maria;
tel. +39 0771 809 835.

## SIGHTS
Neoclassical harbour; Chiaia di Luna beach.

# egadi and aeolian islands

# marettimo

## TRANSPORTATION
BY PLANE Frequent flights to Sicily's two main airports in Palermo and Fontanarossa. Infrequent services to

Trapani (100 km from Palermo).
BY FERRY Siremar ferries and hydrofoils run from Trapani (20-60 minutes by hydrofoil and 1-2 hours by ferry).

## HOTELS
No hotels, but ask at the harbour for the addresses of various homestays.

## RESTAURANTS
IL VELIERO,
Via Umberto 22;
tel. +39 0923 923 195.

## FESTIVALS
La Mattanza takes place in late May or early June.

## SIGHTS
East and West Harbours; clifftop walk; La Mattanza.

# favignana

## TRANSPORTATION
BY PLANE Frequent flights to Sicily's two main airports in Palermo and Fontanarossa. Infrequent services to Trapani (100 km from Palermo).
BY FERRY Siremar ferries and hydrofoils run from Trapani (20-60 minutes by hydrofoil and 1-2 hours by ferry). In the summer Ustica Lines run a hydrofoil service between Trapani-Favignana-Ustica-Naples (Favignana to Naples takes about 6 hours).

## HOTELS
AEGUSA HOTEL & RESTAURANT,
Via Garibaldi 11;

tel. +39 0923 922 430.
VILLA MARGHERITA,
Casette nel verde;
tel. +39 0923 921 501;
www.villamargherita.it.

## RESTAURANTS
EGADI,
Via Cristoforo Colombo 17;
tel. +39 0923 921 232.
LA BETTOLA,
Via Nicotera 47;
tel. +39 0923 921 988.

## FESTIVALS
La Mattanza takes place in late May or early June.

# lipari

## TRANSPORTATION
BY PLANE Both Naples harbours are about 20-30 minutes' drive from Napoli Capodichino airport.
BY FERRY Siremar and SNAV ferries run from Milazzo and from Naples to the Aeolian Islands.
BY BUS Bus service runs from Catania airport to Milazzo for ferry connections.
BY CAR From Rome, take the A1 to Bari, the A16 to Salerno and the A30, following the road markings for the Tangenziale. To reach the harbour of Naples Beverello (ferry and hydrofoil), follow the road markings for the Zona Portuale and continue to the harbour.
BY TRAIN There are four railway stations close to the Naples harbours: Napoli Campi Flegrei (3 km from Mergellina); Napoli Mergellina (200 m from

Mergellina); Napoli Centrale; Napoli Piazza Garibaldi (4 km from Molo Beverello).

## HOTELS
GIARDINO SUL MARE,
Via Maddalena 65;
tel. +39 090 981 1004.
RESIDENCE FIORENTINO,
Via Guiseppe Franza 9;
tel. +39 090 988 0573.
VILLA MELIGUNIS,
Via Marte 7;
tel. +39 090) 981 2426.

## RESTAURANTS
'E PULERA,
Via Diana;
tel. +39 090 981 1158;
www.pulera.it.
LA NASSA,
Via G. Franza 36;
tel. +39 090 981 1319.

## SIGHTS
Castello with fortress walls;
Aeolian Museum.

# vulcano

## TRANSPORTATION
BY PLANE Both Naples harbours are about 20-30 minutes' drive from Napoli Capodichino airport.
BY FERRY Siremar and SNAV (www.snavali.com) ferries run from both Milazzo and Naples to the Aeolian Islands.
BY BUS Bus service runs from Catania airport to Milazzo for ferry connections.
BY CAR From Rome, take the A1 to Bari, the A16 to Salerno and the A30, following

the road markings for the Tangenziale. To reach the harbour of Naples Beverello (ferry and hydrofoil), follow the road markings for the Zona Portuale and continue to the harbour.
BY TRAIN  There are four railway stations close to the Naples harbours: Napoli Campi Flegrei (3 km from Mergellina); Napoli Mergellina (200 m from Mergellina); Napoli Centrale; Napoli Piazza Garibaldi (4 km from Molo Beverello).

HOTELS
LES SABLES NOIRES,
Porto di Ponente;
tel. +39 090 985 0100.

RESTAURANTS
AL CRATERE,
Via Provinciale 31;
tel. +39 090 985 2045

SIGHTS
Hike around the rim of the crater.

# islands of the istrian and dalmatian coast

## brijuni

TRANSPORTATION
BY PLANE  Croatia Airlines (www.croatianairlines.com) schedules seasonal flights to Pula airport (6 km from the centre of town).

BY FERRY  Ferries leave from fishing village of Fazana (15 minutes).
BY BOAT  Boat trips available at Pula harbour.
BY BUS  Local buses from Pula to Fazana leave from Istarske brigade.

HOTELS
HOTEL KARMEN;
tel. +385 052 525 400.
HOTEL NEPTUN-ISTRA;
tel. +385 052 525 100.

RESTAURANTS
Hotels are the only places where food is available.

SIGHTS
Temple of Apollo; exquisite woodlands.

## dugi otok

TRANSPORTATION
BY PLANE  The nearest airport is Zadar-Zemunik (www.zadar-airport.hr).
BY FERRY  In the summer, there are two daily ferries to Dugi Otok, leaving from Zadar and arriving at either Sali or Brbinj. There are also weekly ferries and hydrofoils from Ancona to Brbinj. Tickets are available from Jadrolinija (www.jadrolinija.hr) or Jadroagent.
BY BUS  There are no buses on the island, so a car is essential.
BY TRAIN  Zadar is connected by railway to Zagreb and the rest of Europe.

HOTELS
HOTEL SALI,
Adresa bb, Sali;

tel. +385 023 377 049.

RESTAURANTS
HOTEL SALI and a few harbourside cafés are the only places to eat.

FESTIVALS
The Saljske Uzance festival takes place in Sali in the first week of August (open-air concerts, drinking and feasting).

## hvar

TRANSPORTATION
BY PLANE  Croatia Airlines (www.croatianairlines.com) schedule flights to Split airport (20 km northwest of town between Kastela and Trogir).
BY FERRY  For foot passengers, there is a daily Split–Vela Luka–Lastovo ferry that stops at Hvar town and daily catamarans from Split between mid-May and mid-September. Cars can be taken on Split–Stari Grad ferry. In the summer, there are also ferries from Ancona (in Italy) to Stari Grad and Dvrenik to Sucuraj.
BY BUS  Local buses travel between the ferry pier and the bus station in Hvar Town every hour.
BY TRAIN  Split's train station is close to the main harbourfront road, Obala kneza Domagoja, where all the ferry and hydrofoil berths are located.

HOTELS
HOTEL DELFIN,
Fabrika bb;
tel. +385 021 742 168.
HOTEL PALACE,
Trg svetog Stjepana bb;

tel. +385 021 741 966.
HOTEL SLAVIJA,
Obala oslobodenja bb;
tel. +385 021 741 820.

RESTAURANTS
DEVI, on the corner of Duska Roic and
Puckog Ustanka.
MACONDO (seafood), second alleyway on
the right of Matije Ivanica.
MARINERO, Vinka Pribojevica.

SIGHTS
Citadel; Franciscan Monastery;
Dominican Monastery.

# vis

TRANSPORTATION
BY PLANE Croatia Airlines
(www.croatianairlines.com) schedule
flights to Split airport (20 km northwest of
town between Kastela and Trogir).
BY FERRY Ferries run between Split and
Vis Town (once or twice daily). In the
summer, there are two weekly ferries
from Ancona.
BY TRAIN Split's train station is close to
the main harbourfront road, Obala kneza
Domagoja, where all the ferry and
hydrofoil berths are located.

HOTELS
PANSION AS,
Korzo 16;
tel. +385 021 711 474.
PAULA,
Petra Hektorovica 2;
tel. +385 021 711 362.
HOTEL TAMARIS,

Obala Sv. Jurja 30;
tel. +385 021 711 350.

RESTAURANTS
PAULA,
Petra Hektorovica 2;
tel. +385 021 711 362.
POJODA,
Don C. Marasovica 8;
tel. +385 021 711 575.
VATRICA,
Obala kralja Kresimira IV 13;
tel. +385 021 711 022.

FESTIVALS
On 6 December, Sveti Nikola (St. Nicholas's
Day), the islanders haul a fishing boat up
to the Benedictine Monastery and set it
alight.

SIGHTS
Vis Harbour; Kut; Blue Grotto on
neighbouring Bisevo.

# korcula

TRANSPORTATION
BY PLANE Croatia Airlines
(www.croatianairlines.com) schedule
flights to Split airport (20 km northwest of
town between Kastela and Trogir).
BY FERRY The main Rijeka–Dubrovnik
ferry stops at the harbour of Korcula Town.
There are also daily local ferries between
Split and Vela Luka, at the western end of
the Korcula and between Orebic and
Domince (3 km south of Korcula Town).
BY BUS The daily bus service from
Dubrovnik crosses over from the mainland
via the car ferry from Orebic. Local buses

travel between the Inkobrod shipyard in
Domince and Korcula town.

HOTELS
HOTEL KORCULA,
Obala Vinka Paletina bb;
tel. +385 020 711 078.
HOTEL LIBURNA,
Obala Hrvatskih Mornara bb;
tel. +385 020 726 006.
HOTEL PARK,
Setaliste Frana krsinica bb;
tel. +385 020 726 004.

RESTAURANTS
ADIO MARE,
Svetog Roka;
tel. +385 020 711 253.
GRADSKI PODRUM,
Trg Antuna i Stjepana Radica;
tel. +385 020 711 202.
MARINERO,
ul. Marka Andrijica;
tel. +385 020 711 170.

FESTIVALS
The Moreska sword dance, on weekdays
throughout the summer, leads up to
St. Theodore's Day on 29 September.

SIGHTS
House of Marco Polo, St. Mark's cathedral,
Bishop's Treasury.

# greek islands

## corfu

### TRANSPORTATION
BY PLANE  The airport is 2 km south of the city centre.
BY FERRY  Regular ferry services from Italy, Igoumenitsa and Patra (mainland) and Paxi dock at the New Port (Neo Limani): Adriatica, ANEK, Fragline, Minoan, Strintzis and Ventouris.  The Petrakis agency also runs hydrofoils from Paxi and Igoumenitsa.
BY BUS  Islandwide green bus service is based on Avramiou (service stops by 8 p.m.) and suburban blue bus service is based in Platia San Rocco (service stops by 10 p.m.).

### HOTELS
HOTEL ARCADION,
Kapodhistriou 44;
tel. +30 26610 37670.
BELLA VENEZIA,
Zambeli Str. 4;
tel. +30 26610 46500.
HERMES,
Markora 14;
tel. +30 26610 39304.

### RESTAURANTS
MOURAYIA,
Arseniou 15–17;
tel. +30 26610 38313.
ORESTES,
Xenophondox Stratigou, Mandouki.
REX,
Kapodistriou Str. 66;
tel. +30 26610 39649.

### FESTIVALS
Spectacular Easter Week celebrations; Patron Saint Spiridion is paraded on Palm Sunday, 11 August and first Sunday in November; 23 August, Gastouri Festival; 27 July, Aharavi Festival.

### SIGHTS
Perouladhes beach; Corfu old town, especially Old Fort, new Fort, Byzantine Museum, Liston Arcade; Church of Ayios Spyridhon.

## zakynthos

### TRANSPORTATION
BY PLANE  There is usually a daily flight from Athens to Zakynthos main airport.
BY FERRY  There are eight ferries a day from Killini to the main port in Zakynthos Town and two ferries a day from the port of Pesada on Kefallonia to the village of Skinari.
BY BOAT  Day-trips around the island start at the port in Zakynthos Town and visit the Blue Caves, Shipwreck Bay and Cape Keri.
BY BUS  If arriving in Skinari from Kefallonia, there is only one bus a day to Zakynthos Town (at 3 p.m.). There are no buses from the airport to Zakynthos Town. Local buses can be caught at the bus station in Zakynthos Town, one block behind the seafront

### HOTELS
HOTEL APOLLO,
Tertseti 30;
tel. +30 26950 42838.
HOTEL PALATINO,
Kolokotroni Str. 10;
tel. +30 26950 27780.
STRADA MARINA,
Lomvardou Str. 14;
tel. +30 26950 42761.

### RESTAURANTS
MANTALENA,
seafront, 1km east of Alykes;
tel. +30 26950 83487.

### SIGHTS
Shipwreck Bay; Blue Caves; Monastery of Anafonitria.

## mykonos

### TRANSPORTATION
BY PLANE  Olympic Airways and Aegean Cronus Airlines schedule daily flights from Athens to Mykonos airport.
BY FERRY  Ferries and hydrofoils arrive at the jetty in Tourlos (1 km north of Mykonos Town). There are also boats and car ferries from Athens and Rafina, which call at the islands of Andros, Siros and Tinos (taking 5–6 hours by ferry, 2–3 hours by catamaran).
BY BUS  Regular buses run from the north bus station (to Tourlos, Ayios Stefanos, Elia and Ano Mera) and the south bus station (to beaches in the south).

### HOTELS
BELVEDERE HOTEL;
tel. +30 22890 25122.
SEMELI HOTEL,
Rohan;
tel. +30 22890 27466.

TERRA MARIA,
Kaloyera 18;
tel. +30 22890 24212.

## RESTAURANTS
ANTONINI'S,
Plateia Manto, Mykonos Town;
tel. +30 22890 22319.
CHEZ KATRIN,
Nikiou, Mykonos Town;
tel. +30 22890 22169.
KASTRO,
Little Venice, Mykonos Town;
tel. +30 22890 23072.

## FESTIVALS
30 June, 26 July, 15 August, 26 September,
6 December, Mykonos Town; 6 September,
27 December, Ag Stephanos; 15 August,
Ano Mera.

## SIGHTS
Excursions to nearby island of Delos with
its acropolois; Paraportiani church;
Alefkandhra (Little Venice).

# santorini

## TRANSPORTATION
BY PLANE  Olympic Airways and Aegean
Cronus Airlines schedule daily flights from
Athens to Santorini airport at Monolithos.
In the summer it is also possible to fly from
Thessaloniki.
BY FERRY  Ferries run from Athens to
Ormos Athinios port (9–10 hours).
BY BOAT  From April until October, boat
trips travel between Santorini's northern
ports (Skala Firas and Ia) and Paros, Naxos,
Ios and Crete.

BY BUS  Regular buses connect Fira to
Santorini airport and Athinios.

## HOTELS
HOTEL CYCLADES,
Karteradhos;
tel. +30 22860 24543.
HOTEL LOUCAS,
Caldera View, Fira;
tel. +30 22860 22480.
MANOS APARTMENTS,
Firostefani;
tel. +30 22860 23202.

## RESTAURANTS
ARIS RESTAURANT,
Hotel Loucas, Fira;
tel. +30 22860 22480.
KOUTOUKI,
25 Martiou;
tel. +30 22860 22168.
NIKOLAS,
Erythrou Stavrou;
tel. +30 22860 25400.

## FESTIVALS
Classical music festival in August/
September; 20 July, Ilias Festival; 15
August, Summer Festival.

## SIGHTS
Minoan ruins near Akrotiri; view of Fira and
the caldera from Skaros ruins; Fira
Archaeological Museum.

# symi

## TRANSPORTATION
BY PLANE  Regular flights to Rhodes
airport.

BY FERRY  A daily ferry (2 hours),
catamaran and hydrofoil (55 minutes) run
from Mandhraki in Rhodes Town to Symi.
BY BUS  Local green bus service travels
between Yialos and Pedhi via Horio.

## HOTELS
HOTEL ALIKI,
Akti G. Gennimata;
tel. +30 22460 71665.
HOTEL FIONA,
top of kali Strata;
tel. +30 22460 72088.
HOTEL NIREUS,
Yialos, Pedi Bay;
tel. +30 22460 72400-3.

## RESTAURANTS
TO AMONI,
inland side of main platia,
Yialos.
O MERAKLIS,
Gialos;
tel. +30 22460 71003.
MYTHOS, south quay, Yialos;
tel. +30 22860 71488;
www.mythos-simi.com.

## FESTIVALS
24 June, 15 July, 23 July, 8 August, cultural
festivals; 8 November, Feast of Archangels
Michael and Gabriel (at Taxiarhis
Monastery).

## SIGHTS
Hatziagapitos Mansion; Horio Museum;
Monastery of Taxiarhis Mihail Panormitis
(southern tip).

# rhodes

## TRANSPORTATION
BY PLANE  The airport is 13 km southwest of Rhodes Town.
BY FERRY  Ferries leave from Kolona harbour. Local boats and hydrofoils leave from Mandrakhi yacht harbour.

## HOTELS
HOTEL ANDREAS,
Omirou 28;
tel. +30 22410 34156.
MARCO POLO MANSION
Ayiou Fanouriou 42;
tel. +30 22410 25562.

## RESTAURANTS
ALATOPIPERO,
Michail Petridi 76;
tel. +30 22410 65494.
PALIA ISTORIA,
Mitropoleos 108;
tel. +30 22410 32421.

## SIGHTS
Lindhos Citadel; Rhodes old town, including Palace of Grand Masters, Ottoman Tea-house, Byzantine Museum.

# tunisia

## djerba

## TRANSPORTATION
BY PLANE  Regular scheduled flights to Djerba's international airport in the northwest of the island, near Houmt Souk.

BY FERRY  Regular ferries from port of Jorf to Ajim (15 minutes).
BY CAR  From Mareth, drive south for several kilometres on the GP1, then turn off east after the Mareth Line Museum towards Jorf.
BY BUS  Regular local bus services leave from bus station in centre of Houmt Souk.

## HOTELS
HOTEL ARISHA,
36 R Ghazi Mustapha;
tel. +216 75 650384.
HOTEL DAR SALEM,
4179 Sidi Meherz;
tel. +216 75 757667.
HOTEL MARHALA,
Pl hedi Chaker on R Moncef Bey;
tel. +216 75 650146.

## RESTAURANTS
BACCAR,
Pl Hedi Chaker;
tel. +216 75 650708.
RESTAURANT EL HANA,
Pl Mohamed Ali;
tel. +216 75 650568.
LES PALMIERS,
Place d'Algerie, 14 rue Mohamed Ferjani;
tel. +356 75 621324.

## FESTIVALS
Jewish Pilgrimage on Lag beOmer, the 33rd day after Passover begins, to the synagogue of El Ghriba.

## SIGHTS
Fine beaches around Sidi Mahrez; market days in the bazaar of Houmt Souk; Zaouia of Sidi Brahim; Mosquée des Étrangers; El Ghriba synagogue.

# malta

## gozo

## TRANSPORTATION
BY AIR  Helicopter service from Luqa to Xewkija in the summer.
BY FERRY  Ferry from mainland Malta leaves from Cirkewwa and arrives in Mgarr about half an hour later. Takes cars and foot passengers (www.gozochannel.com).

## HOTELS
GOZO FARMHOUSES;
tel. +356 21 558316;
www.gozofarmhouses.com.
LEGEND,
Republic Street, Victoria;
tel. +356 21 558855.
XAGHRA LODGE,
Dun Gorg Preca Street, Xaghra;
tel. +356 21 562362.

## RESTAURANTS
IT-TMUN,
3 Triq Mount, Carmel, Xlendi;
tel. +356 21 551571.
PULENA,
Marina Street, Marsalforn;
tel. +356 21 559777.
RICCARDO,
4 Fosse Street, Victoria.

## FESTIVALS
Carnival in early March; Nadur Holy Week.

## SIGHTS
Prehistoric temples at Ggantija; neo-classical basilica Ta'Pinu.

# bibliography

Arthus-Bertrand, Yann, *The Earth from the Air*, London, 1999

Borg, Victor Paul, *The Rough Guide to Malta & Gozo*, London, 2001

Bousfield, Jonathan, *The Rough Guide to Croatia*, London, 2000

Bowden, Hugh (ed.), *The Times Ancient Civilisations*, London, 2002

Dubin, Marc, *The Rough Guide to the Greek Islands*, London, 2002 (4th edition)

Durrell, Lawrence, *Prospero's Cell*, London, 1945

Durrell, Lawrence, *Reflections on a Marine Venus*, London, 1953

Finley, M. I., *The World of Odysseus*, London, 1956

Gibbon, Edward, *The History of the Decline and Fall of the Roman Empire*, London, 2000 (abridged edition)

Graves, Robert, *The Greek Myths*, London, 1958

Homer, *The Iliad*, many editions

Homer, *The Odyssey*, many editions

Jacobs, Daniel and Peter Morris, *The Rough Guide to Tunisia*, London, 2001 (6th edition)

Maclean, Fitzroy, *Eastern Approaches*, London, 1949

Ottaway, Mark and Hugh Palmer, *The Most Beautiful Villages of Greece*, London, 1998

Perry, Clay and Elizabeth Boleman-Herring, *Vanishing Greece*, London, 1991

Rossi, Guido Alberto, *Italy from the Air*, London, 1993

Tarling, D. H. & M. P. Tarling, *Continental Drift*, London, 1971

Virgil, *The Aeneid*, London, 2003 (revised edition) (trans. and introduction by David West)

# acknowledgments

The photographer would like to thank Gregor Haas, Gigi Haas, Gabi Blaha, Volker Binder, Patrick McCormick, Luisa Capua, Zelda, Abdel Wargui, Joakim Brattlof, IQ lab, all at Marco Polo Mansion, and all those who opened their doors along the way.